Tried and True ESL Lessons
Level 1 Book A

Time Saving Lesson Plans
For Instructors

Barbara Kinney Black

ISBN: 1975963431
ISBN-13: 978-1975963439

DEDICATION

A dedication can only be to my Lord Jesus Christ who is the 'author and finisher of our faith' and the One who directed the writing of this volume.

CONTENTS

Acknowledgments   i

To the Instructor   iii

Scope and Sequence   vi

1 Personal Communication   2

2 The Community   36

3 Let's Eat   62

4 Shopping   94

5 Housing   110

6 Medical   162

Activity Bank   212

Pronunciation   218

Conducting Drills   220

About the Author   222

ACKNOWLEDGMENTS

Special thanks to my husband for his unending patient assistance, his photographic skill, and attention to detail in the editing process. Also for assuming numerous tasks during the writing process.
Heartfelt thanks also to the 'praying ladies' of Pines Baptist Church who provided much needed constant prayer support.

Barbara Kinney Black

Welcome to <u>Tried and True ESL Lessons, Level 1, Book A: Time Saving Lesson Plans for Instructors</u>. I'm so glad you've decided to give us a try. <u>Tried and True</u> is exactly as its name states: **fully developed ESL lesson plans** compiled from 25 years of classroom teaching experience.

What Tried and True ESL Lessons Can Do for You

- Guides the instructor in classroom presentation.
- Eliminates the need for instructors to write a weekly lesson plan.
- **Frees up the instructor** to concentrate on ministry to the students both inside and outside of the classroom.
- Serves as **a model for instructors** and ministries who wish to develop their own customized curriculum designed for their specific ministry environment.

Why Tried and True ESL Lessons Came to Be

First, here's a little background of how <u>Tried and True ESL Lessons</u> came to be. In my church, we prayed for 11 years to be able to begin an ESL ministry to internationals. After waiting for a church building in which to hold classes, we finally received the green light. The ministry began with four volunteers. We taught for six months and averaged 35 students weekly. At the end of the year, two of the volunteers were unable to continue, so the ministry was shelved.

Eighteen months later, the pastor approached me about beginning the ministry again. We knew the **biggest obstacle** was going to be finding volunteers who possessed enough time and expertise to plan quality lesson plans week to week. The pastor expressed surprise that the vast majority of ESL ministries currently depend on teachers to write their own lesson plans weekly. The pastor wondered why ESL teachers should have to write lesson plans while Sunday School teachers usually do not. Then the pastor asked me to write all the lessons for the teachers. Well, I was **a bit put off** and started to protest, but **the Holy Spirit nudged me** and said, "Be quiet and listen." The pastor made his case, and by the end of our meeting, I heard myself agreeing to write four levels of lesson plans weekly.

As soon as we announced the ministry training workshop, 40 volunteers signed up to attend training. At the completion of the training, 35 trained volunteers signed on to the ministry. **Most had little or no teaching experience**, but were willing to teach since a lesson plan would be provided to them.

What a **fantastic experience**! We soon had six levels of classes with 145 students attending weekly. Yes, it was a lot of work for me, but what rewards to **see volunteers learning to teach** and reach out in ministry to internationals. Incidentally, as a result, two volunteers became ESL teachers in addition to their church ministry.

What's in Level 1, Book A

Most church based ESL ministries meet one time per week for a 1 ½ - 2 hour session. These sessions generally follow the public school calendar from Labor Day to Memorial Day with a Christmas break. This totals about 30 weeks of instruction. The Fall semester has about 13 weeks and the Spring semester about 16 weeks. **Book A with its 13 lessons** is a perfect fit for the Fall semester, but can be used at any time of year.

Lessons utilize a **functional approach** to language learning with an emphasis on simulating real life language situations. Students learn real language through a lot of **speaking and communication practice activities**. All lessons contain relevant material practical for everyday life in an English speaking country. They also contain a **biblical principle** related to the content of the lesson.

The **student book** is titled, Tried and True ESL Lessons, Level 1, Book A. **Lessons are 8-10 pages** in length and feature vocabulary supported by pictures for comprehension, speaking, listening, grammar, pronunciation, and communication practice activities. There are also assignments in each lesson to do outside the classroom designed to reinforce language learning.

Tried and True ESL Lessons, Level 1, Book A: Time Saving Lesson Plans for Instructors, features an **Activity Bank** to guide instructors in **how to conduct** the Let's Practice communication activities. Any additional materials needed are very minimal and easily accessible. An alternate is usually suggested, as well. **Techniques** for presenting pronunciation and drilling vocabulary are included.

Since many ministries and students tend to operate on a limited budget, every consideration was made to keep the cost of Tried and True ESL Lessons at the absolute bare minimum. Therefore, both instructor and student editions are published in black and white in order to make the program **very affordable**. For this reason, please note this is NOT a reproducible text.

Tried and True ESL Lessons offers an additional Resource Manual of **full color photos** of the vocabulary for comprehension which appear in both the student and instructor editions in **black and white**. This **optional <u>Resource Manual</u> of color photos** is designed to support comprehension and further enhance the instructor's presentation and students' clear comprehension.

So, once again, welcome to <u>Tried and True ESL Lessons</u>. **I pray** your experience with this curriculum will be a rewarding one whether you are a **brand new instructor, or a seasoned veteran**. To God be the glory!

Because of Him and them,

Barbara K. Black
M.S. T.E.S.O.L.
email: bekblack19@gmail.com
FB: Tried and True ESL Resources
Web: TriedandTrueESLResources.com

Barbara Kinney Black

Tried and True ESL Lessons Level 1 - Book A

Time Saving Lesson Plans for Instructors

By Barbara K. Black

Scope and Sequence

Unit-Lesson	Topic	Skills	Grammar
		Personal Communication	
1-1	Introductions	Introducing self & others	To Be; WH-Questions
1-2	The Family	Describing family members	WHO Questions; To Be; Subject Pronouns
		The Community	
2-1	Locations of Places	Describing locations of places in the community	Prepositions of Location
2-2	Emergencies	Reporting emergencies to 911	Present Progressive
		Let's Eat	
3-1	Supermarket	Categorizing foods by Department	Contractions
3-2	Food Packaging	Describing food packaging & measurements	Count/Noncount Nouns; Using There Is/There are; Some & Any
		Shopping	
4-1	Clothing Size & Fit	Describing Clothing Fit	Too + Adjectives

Unit-Lesson	Topic	Skills	Grammar
		Housing	
5-1	Choosing Housing	Describing types of housing & housing features	Articles A and AN
5-2	Moving	Describing positioning of home furnishings	Demonstratives; Where + Do
5-3	Cleaning House	Identifying cleaning products tasks	Imperative Commands; Prepositions of Location
		Medical	
6-1	The Body	Identifying human body parts	Possessive Adjectives
6-2	Personal Hygiene	Describing daily personal hygiene actions	Simple Present Tense Present Progressive Tense
6-3	The Pharmacy	Describing common physical Ailments & Identifying OTC Medicines	Using Have; Can & Can't

Welcome to
Tried and True ESL Lessons
Level 1 Book A

Time Saving Lesson Plans
for Instructors

UNIT 1 – PERSONAL COMMUNICATION - LESSON 1 – INTRODUCTIONS
STUDENT BOOK PAGE 1

A. Prayer for Students & Self

B. Lesson Objective and Functions:
• Introducing self and others

C. Grammar Structures:
• To Be Verb
• Asking WH-Questions

D. Biblical Reference or Principles:
• Exodus 33:11 – God said to Moses, "I am the Lord."

E. Materials & Preparation
• Large map of the world, name badge for teacher, blank name badges and markers. Alternately, use map in book.
• For the activity How Do You Spell That?: one set of alphabet flash cards. Alternately, write the alphabet on the board.
• For the activity Where Are You From?: large map of the world or copy the map from the book and place on the board; repositionable map markers made from stick-on notes in various colors or small papers and tacky tape

Introduction
Have students open to Unit 1 – Personal Communication – Lesson 1 – Introductions and Personal Communication.
Introduce yourself. Say: "My name is _____" while pointing to the name badge.
Ask one student: "What's your name?" When student responds, give student a blank name badge and marker to write his/her name. Repeat with all students.

Introduce New Vocabulary
Drill and demonstrate the 5 pictures. Repeat at least 5 times.
Demonstrate firm hand shake and the importance of looking into the eyes of the person you are shaking hands with. Demonstrate/explain that men must shake hands with other men. It is optional for women, but professional for a woman to extend her hand first to shake. Particularly in the business setting it is important for women to shake hands with men and with other women.
Also demonstrate the firm hand shake vs. the "limp fish" hand shake. Demonstrate/explain the importance of the firm hand shake.
Demonstrate/explain how long you look into the other person's eyes. It's not a stare, but a brief, friendly glance, and then look elsewhere. Also explain what is communicated by NOT looking into the eyes: rejection, distrust, etc.

UNIT 1
PERSONAL COMMUNICATION
LESSON 1 – INTRODUCTIONS

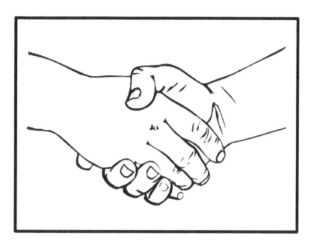

shake hands

M-A-R-I-A

spell

Registration

Name: _Barbara_

Country _Cuba_

registration form

**HELLO,
my name is:**
Barbara

name

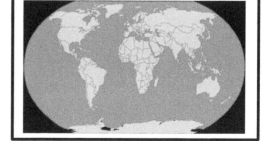

country from

UNIT 1 – PERSONAL COMMUNICATION - LESSON 1 – INTRODUCTIONS
STUDENT BOOK PAGE 2

1. Use the map. Point out where you are from. Say: "I'm from ____." Then ask: "Where are you from?" Help students say, "I'm from____" and point out their countries on the map.

2. Say: "Today we are going to learn how to introduce ourselves."

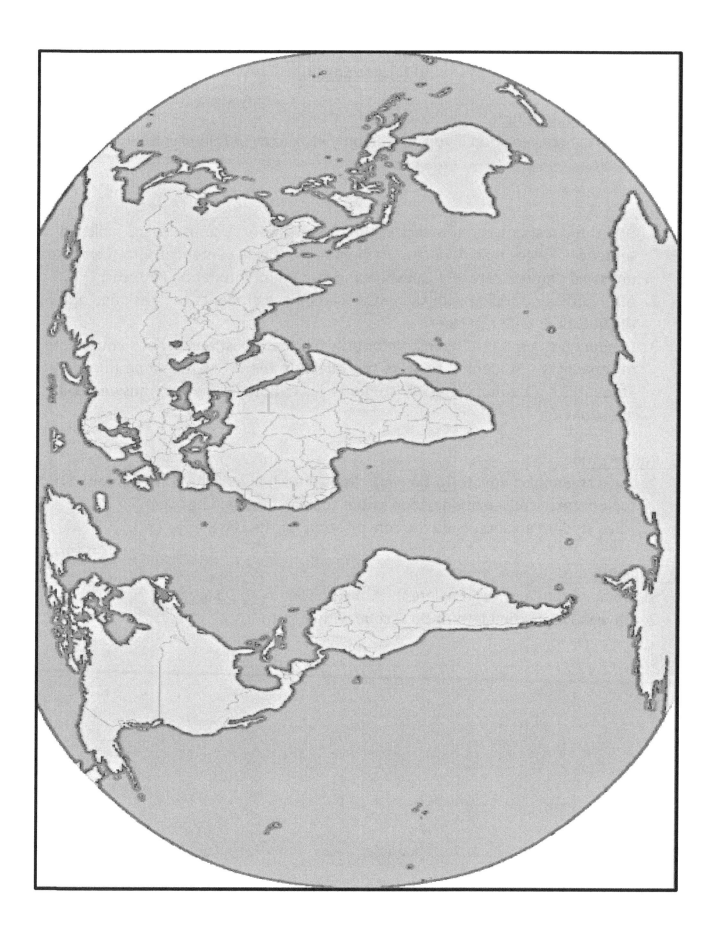

UNIT 1 – PERSONAL COMMUNICATION - LESSON 1 – INTRODUCTIONS
STUDENT BOOK PAGE 3

Time to Speak

A. Introduce Conversation

Pantomime the conversation if you are the only instructor or role play if two instructors are available.

B. Drills

1. Drill the questions and answers in the conversation. Use backward build up for sentences longer than 4 words. Remember to divide sentences into their sound units and demonstrate WH-Question and Statement Intonation Patterns.
2. After sufficient drilling with the whole class, have students both ask and answer the questions with a partner.
3. Conduct a chain drill. The instructor asks the first question, 'What's your name?' of Student 1. Student 1 answers the question then asks the same question to Student 2. Continue until all students have both asked and answered all 3 questions.

C. Conversation

1. Have students complete _To Do First._ Repeat each line of the conversation. Strive for a normal, conversational tone rather than an oral reading tone.
2. Have student volunteers do the conversation for the class.

D. Substitutions

1. Demonstrate how to complete the Substitutions in _To Do Second._
2. Have students complete _To Do Second_ with a partner.

Time to Speak

To Do First: Repeat the conversation after the instructor.

What's Your Name?
Speaker A: New Student   Speaker B: Instructor

1.A.   Hi. I want to register for class.
   1.B.   O.K. What's your name?
2.A.   My name is **Juan Roque**.
   2.B.   How do you spell that?
3.A.   **J-U-A-N   R-O-Q-U-E**.
   3.B.   Where are you from?
4.A.   I'm from **Venezuela**.
   4.B.   Nice to meet you.

To Do Second: Speak with a partner. Change the <u>underlined words</u> in the conversation for the Substitutions in No. 1-3 below.

Substitution No. 1

2.A.   My name is Rosangela Morado.
3.A.   R-O-S-A-N-G-E-L-A   M-O-R-A-D-O.
4.A.   I'm from Brazil.

Substitution No. 2

2.A.   My name is Ming Lee.
3.A.   M-I-N-G   L-E-E.
4.A.   I'm from China.

Substitution No. 3

2.A.   My name is Fredeline Francois.
3.A.   F-R-E-D-E-L-I-N-E   F-R-A-N-C-O-I-S.
4.A.   I'm from Haiti.

UNIT 1 – PERSONAL COMMUNICATION - LESSON 1 – INTRODUCTIONS
STUDENT BOOK PAGE 4

<u>Grammar Foundation</u>

A. Introduce the Grammar Foundation by reading the information under "To Be Verb".
Give other example sentences for: How we are, Who we are, and Where we are. Ask
for other example sentences from students.

B. Complete *To Do First* by having students repeat each of the Statements after the
instructor. Repeat each one 5-6 times. After each set (singular and plural forms),
review.

C. Complete *To Do Second* and *To Do Third*.

D. Introduce the Grammar Foundation "Asking WH-Questions". Point out the different
Question Words and what type of answer for each question word.

Grammar Foundation

To Do First:
Repeat each sentence after the instructor.

1. To Be Verb

The Be Verb is used to describe State of Being. We use it to describe (1) how we are, or (2) who we are, or (3) a place we are at. For example:

How we are:	Who we are	Where we are:
I am sick.	I am a teacher.	I am at the library.
You are happy.	You are a student.	You are at McDonalds.
She is hungry.	She is a mother.	She is at work.

Statements

Subject + Be Verb			Subject + Be Verb		
Singular Forms			**Plural Forms**		
I	am	a teacher.	We	are	tired.
You	are	a student.	We	are	friends.
He	is	well.	You	are	in Chicago.
He	is	an uncle.	They	are	absent.
She	is	at church.	They	are	sisters.
It	is	raining.			

To Do Second:
Speak to a partner. Make statements about yourself, your family, and other students.

To Do Third:
Repeat each question and answer after the instructor.

2. Asking WH-Questions

WH-Questions are questions which begin with a question word: who, what, where, when, why, or how. The answer gives specific information.

Question Word	The Answer is About
Who	a person
What	a thing

UNIT 1 – PERSONAL COMMUNICATION - LESSON 1 – INTRODUCTIONS
STUDENT BOOK PAGE 5

E. Have students repeat the WH-Question Examples and Answers after the instructor.

F. After sufficient drilling, role play students answering the questions under the Singular Forms (all except for the 'Who is he?' and 'Where is she?' questions).

G. Finish with drilling the Plural Forms WH-Questions and Answers.

Let's Practice

A. Conduct the Let's Practice Activity 1. How Do You Spell That?

Prepare in advance. Materials: set of alphabet flash cards (create with 4x6 index cards and draw one capital letter on each card with a broad tip marker) or write the alphabet on the board.
   1. Have students repeat the alphabet using flash cards.
   2. Repeat alphabet using the Alphabet Chant (military 'sound off' call and response chant) or you may consider something similar to the A-B-C song that children use to learn the alphabet. NOTE: Remember we are teaching adults so it may be better to come up with an alternative song rather than use the familiar childrens' A-B-C song.
   3. Use the Conversation and Substitutions and spell the names together.
   4. Have students each write their names on the board using large block letters.
   5. Ask questions: "How do you spell Maria's name?" Students spell from board.
   6. Students ask and answer the questions.

B. Conduct the Let's Practice Activity 2. Where Are You From?
   1. Prepare in advance.
   2. Materials: use a large map of the world or copy the map from the book and place it on the board, repositionable map markers made from repositionable stick-on notes in various colors (consider coloring 1 ½ "x 2" Post It notes with different colored markers, or use Post It Flags, or color small pieces of paper with markers and affix them to the map with tacky tape).
   3. Teach statement: "Where are you from?"

Where	a place
When	time
Why	the reason
How	the process

WH-Question + Be Verb			Answers
Singular Forms			
What	is	your name?	My name is Barbara.
What	is	your address?	My address is 2110 N.W. 152 Street.
Who	is	he?	He is my brother.
Where	is	she?	She is at school.
Who	is	your friend?	His name is Rolando.
When	is	your class?	It's at 7:00.
How old		are you?	I'm 25 years old.
Where		are you from?	I'm from Haiti.
Plural Forms			
What		are those flowers?	They are roses.
Who		are those people?	They are new students.
Where		are those students from?	They are from China.
When		are John and Jerry coming back?	They are coming back in January.

Let's Practice

1. How Do You Spell That?

1. Speak with a partner. Use the Conversation and Substitutions. Practice spelling the names.
2. Write your name on the board with large letters.
3. The instructor will ask students to spell names.

2. Where Are You From?

1. Write your name on a small paper.
2. The instructor will ask you, "Where are you from?" Answer the question, for example, "I'm from Cuba."

UNIT 1 – PERSONAL COMMUNICATION - LESSON 1 – INTRODUCTIONS
STUDENT BOOK PAGE 6

1. Have one student ask the instructor, "Where are you from?" Instructor responds, "I'm from _____" while placing a repositionable map marker on the map.
2. Distribute repositionable map markers to each student. Student 1 asks Student 2, "Where are you from?" Student 2 responds, "I'm from _____" and places his/her repositionable map marker on the map. Continue until all students have asked and answered the question.
3. While students are naming their countries, instructor lists their countries on the board.
4. Students spell country names.

C. Conduct the Let's Practice Activity 3. Interview Line-Up

1. Create two equal lines of students facing each other about 2' apart. Designate Line A and B.
2. Instructor gives an interview topic/question for Line A to interview their partner in Line B.
3. When all have completed the interview, the student at the end of Line A moves to the opposite end of Line A while other students in Line A shift one place over. Line B does not move. All students now face a new partner.
4. Instructor gives a new interview topic/question. Line B begins the interview.
5. Continue shifting Line A until all students have interviewed each other.

Questions: Use the questions from the Conversation drilled earlier. Students answer with their own information. Also use questions from the Grammar Foundation.

D. Conduct the Let's Practice activity 4. Play Beat the Cat with the puzzle sentence from Exodus 6:2: "God said to Moses, "I am the Lord."
See the example below of how to conduct Beat the Cat using the puzzle sentence 'God is love':

1. Write the letters of the alphabet across the top of the board.
2. Draw lines to represent the letters of each word in the puzzle sentence. For example:

    ____ _____   ___   ___ _____

3. Students take turns guessing **consonants** only.
4. Fill in the guessed consonants that appear in the puzzle. For example:

    ____   ___   D___   ___   S___

5. For consonants guessed that do NOT appear in the puzzle, begin drawing a cat, one body part per incorrect consonant, in the following order: head, body, face, whiskers, ears, tail. The addition of the tail indicates the teacher has won! Avoid this by adding paws to the cat if needed!
6. Continue until all consonant spaces are filled in.
7. Students guess which vowels fill the remaining spaces in the puzzle. Fill in their correct vowel guesses. For example: G O D I S L O V E. Students read the completed puzzle.

   3. Put your name on the map by your country.
   4. Spell the country names.

3. Interview Line-Up

   1. Follow the instructor's directions. Make a line with other students.
   2. Ask questions to other students. The instructor will give you the questions.

4. Play Beat the Cat

   1. This game is like the TV show Wheel of Fortune. The instructor will put a puzzle on the board.
   2. Students take turns guessing consonants.
   3. If the consonant is in the puzzle, the instructor will write it on the line. If the consonant is NOT in the puzzle, the instructor will draw part of a cat.
   4. Continue until only vowels are left in the puzzle.

UNIT 1 – PERSONAL COMMUNICATION - LESSON 1 – INTRODUCTIONS
STUDENT BOOK PAGE 7

<u>Review Exercises</u>

<u>1. Complete the Questions – Answer the Questions</u>
Answer Key – answers in bold

1. What's your name?   **[students write their names]**

2. Where are you from?   **[students write their countries]**

<u>2. Correct the Mistakes</u>
Answer Key – answers in bold

1. What your name?   *What's your name.*

2. What are you from?   *Where are you from?*

3. Where the instructor from?   *Where is the instructor from?*

4. I'm from Spanish.   *I'm from [name of country]*

5. My name is Brazil.   *My name is [student's name]*

6. The instructor's name is Haiti.   *The instructor's name is [instructor name]*

Review Exercises

1. Complete the Questions – Answer the Questions

1. Complete the questions.
2. Answer the questions.

Questions	Answers
1. What's your name?	*My name*
2. Where	

2. Correct the Mistakes

1. The sentences under Wrong Sentence are incorrect. Find the mistake.
2. Write the Correct Sentence.

Wrong Sentence	**Correct Sentence**
1. What your name?	*What's your name.*
2. What are you from?	
3. Where the instructor from?	
4. I'm from Spanish.	
5. My name is Brazil.	
6. The instructor's name is Haiti.	

UNIT 1 – PERSONAL COMMUNICATION - LESSON 1 – INTRODUCTIONS
STUDENT BOOK PAGE 8

3. Circle the Hidden Words
Answer Key – answers in bold

A S D F G H **N A M E** K L I Y N M E N W Q N B B Y U N E A

N Y U I Y T E N W E T N B G Y N E W T **L A N G U A G E** U

G U Y N M I N **C L A S S** Y I O Y B A S D B N Y I Y T Q X

S P E L L H N Y I O P Y B V C X Z S E W Q N I Y I O P N

W N I O H N I O P U U W Q W E **W E L C O M E** Y N R I O W

Y U T I O P Y E R B Q U N I O B M B E V C O **S P E A K** G

3. Circle the Hidden Words

Circle the words in the puzzle.

NAME   SPEAK   SPELL   LANGUAGE   CLASS   WELCOME

A S D F G H N A M E K L I Y N M E N W Q N B B Y U N E A

N Y U I Y T E N W E T N B G Y N E W T L A N G U A G E U

G U Y N M I N C L A S S Y I O Y B A S D B N Y I Y T Q X

S P E L L H N Y I O P Y B V C X Z S E W Q N I Y I O P N

W N I O H N I O P U U W Q W E W E L C O M E Y N R I O W

Y U T I O P Y E R B Q U N I O B M B E V C O S P E A K G

4. Introduce Yourself

1. Introduce yourself to 3 people this week. Tell your name and where you are from.
2. Ask their name and where they are from.
3. Tell the class about it next week.

UNIT 1 – PERSONAL COMMUNICATION - LESSON 1 – INTRODUCTIONS
STUDENT BOOK PAGE 9

<u>5. Use the Grammar</u>
Answer Key – answers in bold

Complete the sentences with the correct form of the BE Verb.

1. What __***is***__ your name?

2. Where __***are***__ you from?

3. When __***is***__ your interview?

4. We _____***are***_____ hungry.

5. They _____***are***_____ absent.

6. My son _____***is***__ at the library.

7. Where __***are***__ your friends from?

8.   What time _____***is***__ it?

9. It _____***is***__ not raining.

10. They __***are***__ not in class.

Keep up the good work!

5. Use the Grammar

Complete the sentences with the correct form of the BE Verb.

1. What _is_ your name?

2. Where _____ you from?

3. When _____ your interview?

4. We _____ hungry.

5. They _____ absent.

6. My son _____ at the library.

7. Where _____ your friends from?

8. What time _____ it?

9. It _____ not raining.

10. They _____ not in class.

UNIT 1 – PERSONAL COMMUNICTION - LESSON 2 – FAMILY
STUDENT BOOK PAGE 10

A. Prayer for Students & Self

B. Lesson Objective and Functions:
- Identifying family members by relationship

C. Grammar Structures:
- Asking questions with WHO
- BE Verb
- Subject Pronouns

D. Biblical Reference or Principles:
- 1 John 3:1 – See how much the Father has loved us! His love is so great that we are called God's children.

E. Materials & Preparation:
- pictures of students' family
- picture of instructor's family
- koosh ball
- family word cards: write each family word on an individual 4x6 index card

Introduction
1. Show the class a picture of your family. Identify the family members by pointing and saying, "That's my father, Michael." Continue identifying all family members in your photo.
2. Students should have been reminded in the last class to bring a picture of their family. For those who did, ask questions: "Who is that?"
3. Alternately, Students who did not bring a photo should show a picture on their phone or take a moment to draw stick figures for each member of their family and label them with names.
4. Say: "Today we are going to talk about our families."

Introduce New Vocabulary
1. Have students open to Unit 1 – Personal Communication; Lesson 2 – The Family.
2. Point out this tree is about Maria's family. Identify each family member in relation to Maria.
3. Introduce the family words in Maria's Family Tree using a repetition drill. Repeat each word 5-6 times.
4. Ask students questions about their own family, for example:
- Are your parents living?
Do you have children? NOTE: The question, "Are you married?" may be too personal. Perhaps let students volunteer that information.

UNIT 1
PERSONAL COMMUNICATION
LESSON 2 – THE FAMILY

MARIA'S FAMILY TREE

UNIT 1 – PERSONAL COMMUNICTION - LESSON 2 – FAMILY
STUDENT BOOK PAGE 11

Time to Speak

A. Complete *To Do First:*
1. Introduce the conversation under Time to Speak. Have students repeat each line after the instructor. Repeat each line 5-6 times. Strive for a normal, conversation tone rather than an oral reading tone.
2. Use backward build up for sentences longer than 4 words. Remember to divide sentences into their sound units.
3. Use correct intonation, stress, and rhythm patterns. Include the following intonation patterns:
- WH-Question intonation
- Statement

B. Have students complete *To Do Second.* Call on individual students to read the conversation after each substitution has been drilled.

C. Have students complete *To Do Third*. Give assistance with additional family words not introduced in the lesson. Allow use of picture dictionaries.

To Do First: Repeat the conversation after the instructor.

This is My Family

1.A.   This is a picture of my family.
   1.B.   Who's that?
2.A.   That's my father, Michael.
   2.B.   And who is she?
3.A.   She is my mother, Monica.
   3.B.   Who is he?
4.A.   He is my husband, Henry.
   4.B.   And who are they?
5.A.   They are my children, Paula and Peter.

To Do Second:
1. Practice the conversation with a partner.
2. Volunteer pairs present their conversations for the class.

To Do Third:
1. Draw a picture of your family or show a picture on your cell phone. Work with a partner.
2. Student 2 asks Student 1, "Who is that?" while pointing to one of the family members in Student 1's picture. Student 1 answers, for example: "She is my daughter."
3. Continue until Student 1 has identified all family members.
4. Repeat the activity with Student 2's family picture.

UNIT 1 – PERSONAL COMMUNICTION - LESSON 2 – FAMILY
STUDENT BOOK PAGE 12

Grammar Foundation

1. Asking Questions with WHO

A. Read the information under Asking Questions with WHO.

B. Complete _To Do First_ by having students repeat each example question and answer after the instructor.

2. Using the Verb To BE

A. Introduce the structure for both Singular Forms and Plural Forms.

B. Have students complete _To Do First_ by repeating each example after the instructor. Repeat each one 5-6 times.

Grammar Foundation

1. Asking Questions with WHO

The question word WHO is used to ask about a person. For example:

Who + Be + Object   Answers

Singular Forms

Who	are	you?	I am Mrs. Black
Who	is	he?	He is my father.
Who	is	she?	She is my mother.
Who	is	Mrs. Black?	She is my sister.
Who	is	your teacher?	Mrs. Black is my teacher.
Who	is	that?	That is my husband.

Plural Forms

| Who | are | you? | We are your students. |
| Who | are | they? | They are my children. |

2. Using the Verb To BE

Use BE to talk about who a person is.

To Do First: Repeat each example sentence after the instructor.

Subject + Be

Singular Forms

I	am	a woman.
You	are	a student.
He	is	my father.
She	is	my wife.
Maria	is	my sister.
John	is	my husband.
Kiki	is	my cat.

Plural Forms

We	are	your students.
You	are	my friends.
They	are	my children.

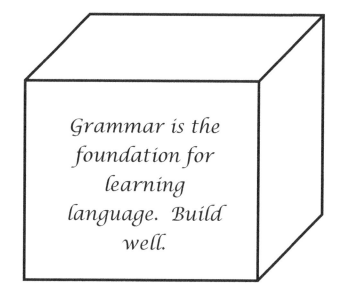

Grammar is the foundation for learning language. Build well.

UNIT 1 – PERSONAL COMMUNICTION - LESSON 2 – FAMILY
STUDENT BOOK PAGE 13

C. Have students complete _To Do Second_ by making statements about their own families.

3. Subject Pronouns

A. Introduce Subject Pronouns by reading the information.

B. Have students complete _To Do_ by repeating each Subject Pronoun after the instructor. Practice saying the Pronouns quickly as a group, for example: I, you, he, she, it, we, you, they.

Practicing Perfect Pronunciation

1. Practicing the Sounds of /t/ and /th/

A. Introduce the sounds by reading the information.

B. Teach how to produce the /t/ sound. Describe the placement of the tongue behind the front teeth. Demonstrate making the /t/ sound. Remember that /t/ is a Voiceless sound, so only the sound of escaping air should be heard.

C. Practice pronouncing the example words: sister and daughter. Add additional /t/ words as desired.

D. Teach how to produce the /th/ sound. Describe the placement of the tongue slightly between the two front teeth. Demonstrate how quickly the tongue is retracted. Explain that it's not rude to show the tongue when producing the /th/ sound. Suggest the use of a mirror to aid in seeing what their tongue is doing. Remember that this /th/ is a Voiceless sound, so only the sound of escaping air should be heard. Also note the sound is not completed until the tongue is retracted back into the mouth.

E. Practice pronouncing the example words: mother, father, brother. Add additional /th/ words as desired.

To Do Second: Students make sentences about their own family.

3. Subject Pronouns
We use SUBJECT PRONOUNS to take the place of a Subject in a sentence. The first time you talk about a person, use the person's name, for example: "This is Maria." The second time you can use the Subject Pronoun, for example: "She is my friend."

To Do: Repeat each Subject Pronoun after the instructor.

Singular Forms	**Plural Forms**
I	we
you	you
he	they
she	
it	

~~ *Practicing Perfect Pronunciation* ~~

1. Practicing the Sounds of /t/ and /th/
The sounds of /t/ as in sister and daughter, and the sound of /th/ as in mother, father, and brother, are said very differently.

To pronounce the /t/ sound, place the tip of the tongue behind the front teeth. Blow out air to pronounce. Let the air push your tongue down.

Repeat after the instructor:
sister   daughter

To produce the /th/ sound, place the tip of the tongue between the teeth and begin to pronounce the /th/ sound. Bring the tongue back into the mouth to finish the sound. You can use a mirror to help see where your tongue is.

Repeat after the instructor:
mother   father   brother

UNIT 1 – PERSONAL COMMUNICTION - LESSON 2 – FAMILY
STUDENT BOOK PAGE 14

2. Practicing the /z/ Sound in Contractions

A. Introduce the Contractions by reading the information.

B. Read the Full Form and Contraction examples.

C. Help students produce the /z/ sound. Demonstrate touching the voice box. If students are having trouble, ask them to produce the sound of a buzzing bee.

Let's Practice
A. Conduct the Let's Practice Activity 1. Dictation
   1. Write each of the family words on the board and assign a number.
   2. Dictate the family words randomly by spelling only.
   3. Students write the dictated letters, then locate the word on the board.
   4. Students write the number of the dictated word.
   5. Go over responses.

B. Conduct the Let's Practice Activity 2. Male/Female Family Words – Categorizing
   1. Practice family word opposites using the koosh ball.
   2. Say a family word, for example: "mother," and toss the ball to a student.
   3. Student catches the ball and states the opposite of mother: "father."
   4. Continue until all have participated.
   5. Alternately, allow students to initiate activity by tossing ball and saying a family word.
   6. Distribute one family word card to each student.
   7. Students mix to find their opposite family member.
   8. Draw two columns on the board labeled "Male" and "Female". Students affix their family name cards to board using tacky tape or scotch tape under the appropriate column.

C. Conduct the Let's Practice Activity 3. Family Pictures – Listening Activity
   1. Have students open their books to the activity.
   2. If two instructors are available, read the transcript Family Pictures Listening Activity, next page. If only one instructor, read the transcript including the number and letter of each line, for example: 1.A., 1.B., etc. The transcript is the Answer Key below. Read the **bold** words.
   3. Students circle the correct response.
   4. Repeat as often as students request.
   5. Students read answers to class.

2. Practicing the /z/ Sound in Contractions

English speakers use contractions—two words put together. Here's some contractions.

<u>Full Form</u>   <u>Contraction</u>

who is   who's

she is   she's

he is   he's

To pronounce the 's on the Contraction, make a /z/ sound. Make the /z/ sound just like the /s/ sound, but vibrate your voice box. Place your hands on your throat (neck) and feel your voice box. When you make the /z/ sound, your voice box will buzz like a bee. This is called vibration.

Practice with the instructor.

1. Dictation

1. The instructor will write the family words on the board.
2. The instructor will spell a family word. Write the letters on your paper.
3. Find the family word on the board. Write the number of the word next to the word you spelled.
4. Check your answers with the class.

2. Male/Female Family Words – Categorizing

1. The instructor will say a family word, for example: "mother." The instructor will throw a ball to Student 1.
2. Student 1 catches the ball and says the opposite of mother, for example: "father."
3. Student 1 throws the ball to the instructor.

3. Family Pictures – Listening Activity

1. Open your book to the Family Pictures Listening Activity page.
2. You will hear some conversations. Circle the word in the [brackets] that you hear.
3. The instructor will read the conversation as many times as students ask.

UNIT 1 – PERSONAL COMMUNICTION - LESSON 2 – FAMILY
STUDENT BOOK PAGE 15

Transcript: Family Pictures Listening Activity

1.A. [**Who's** / Who] that?
    1.B. [That / **That's**] my mother, Melinda.
2.A. And who is [**she** / he]?
    2.B. [He / **She**] is my sister, Moeisha.
3.A. Who are they?
    3.B. They [is / **are**] my three [**children** / childs] Peter, Paul, and Patrick.
4.A. Who [is / **are**] they?
    4.B. They are my [**brothers** / mothers]. His name is [**John** / Tom] and [**his** / hers] name is Tom.
5.A. Who is he?
    5.B. [**He** / She] is my husband, Bernie.
6.A. [**You** / Do] have a nice family.
    6.B. Thank you.

1.A. [Who's / Who] that?

    1.B. [That / That's] my mother, Melinda.

2.A. And who is [she / he]?

    2.B. [He / She] is my sister, Moeisha.

3.A. Who are they?

    3.B. They [is / are] my three [children /   childs] Peter, Paul, and Patrick.

4.A. Who [is / are] they?

    4.B. They are my [brothers / mothers]. His name is

[John / Tom] and [his / hers] name is Tom.

5.A. Who is he?

    5.B. [He / She] is my husband, Bernie.

6.A. [You / Do] have a nice family.

    6.B. Thank you.

UNIT 1 – PERSONAL COMMUNICATION - LESSON 2 – FAMILY
STUDENT BOOK PAGE 16

Conduct the Let's Practice Activity 3. Verse Picture Puzzle
1. This is the biblical principle activity taken from 1 John 3:1: See how much the Father has loved us! His love is so great that we are called God's children.
2. The random order for the pictures shown in the student book is listed below:

See how much (picture No. 6) the Father (picture No. 3) has loved us! (picture No. 5)

His love (picture No. 1) is so great that we are called (picture No. 4) God's children.

(picture No. 2)

A. Direct students to unscramble the verse and put the pictures into correct order.
B. Students read the story.
C. Instructor may choose to comment on the verse's meaning.

3. Verse Picture Puzzle

There are 6 pictures below. They tell a story. Look at and read the pictures.
Number them into correct order. Read for the class.

His love

_____

God's children

_____

the Father

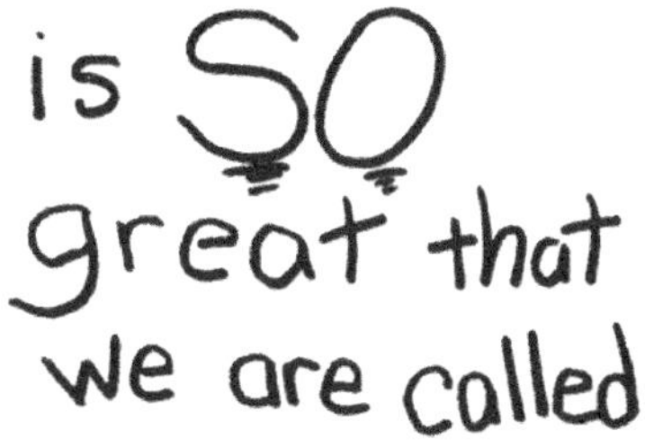

_____

is SO great that we are called

_____

has ♡ us.

_____

how much

_____

UNIT 1 – PERSONAL COMMUNICATION - LESSON 2 – FAMILY
STUDENT BOOK PAGE 17

Review Exercises

Exercises are designed to be completed for homework. Go over instructions so everyone is clear how to complete the activities.

1. Put the Family Words into Alphabetical (A-Z) Order
Review alphabetical order if needed.

Answer Key -

1.	brother	5.	mother
2.	daughter	6.	sister
3.	father	7.	son
4.	husband	8.	wife

2. Complete the Sentences

Answer Key –
1. Who is **he** ?   **He**   is my brother.
2. Who is **she** ?   **She**   is my mother.
3. Who **are** they?   **They**   are my children.
4. Who **is** your teacher? **My**   teacher is **[instructor's name]**.

3. Write the Male and Female Family Words

Answer Key –

	Female		Male
1.	mother	1.	father
2.	sister	2.	brother
3.	wife	3.	son
4.	daughter	4.	husband

Review Exercises

1. Put the Family Words into Alphabetical (A-Z) Order

A. mother   B. father   C. sister   D. brother

E. husband   F. wife   G. son   H. daughter

1. **brother** _____   5. _____

2. _____   6. _____

3. _____   7. _____

4. _____   8. _____

2. Complete the Sentences

1. Who is ___*he*___ ?   _____ is my brother.

2. Who is _____ ?   _____ is my mother.

3. Who _____ they?   _____ are my children.

4. Who _____ your teacher?   _____ teacher is _____.

3. Write the Male and Female Family Words

Female	Male
1. *mother*	1.
2.	2.
3.	3.
4.	4.

Answer Key 1 John 3:1: See how much the Father has loved us! His love is so great that we are called God's children.

4. Write Sentences about your Family

1. _____

2. _____

3. _____

UNIT 2 – THE COMMUNITY - LESSON 1 – LOCATIONS OF PLACES
STUDENT BOOK PAGE 18

A. Prayer for Students & Self

B. Lesson Objective and Functions:
• Inquiring about location of places in the community
• Describing locations of places in the community.

C. Grammar Structures:
• Prepositions of Location: on; on the corner of; across from

D. Biblical Reference or Principles:
• The Kingdom of God is within you

E. Materials & Preparation

Introduction

1. Ask: Where's the drug store? Supermarket? Hospital? Mall? [get student responses]

2. Say: Different countries give directions to locations in different ways. [Tell any stories you know about asking directions in other countries, or tell the following: In San Jose, Costa Rica, when you want to go to the downtown bus station, you get into a taxi and say, "Coca Cola", and the taxi will take you to the bus station. The reason is that the Coca Cola bottling plant USED TO BE next to the bus station.]

3. Ask: How do you give directions or ask for directions in your country?

4. Say: Today we are going to learn how to ask for locations and tell someone where to find places in the community.

Introduce New Vocabulary

1. Have students open to Unit 2 – The Community – Lesson 1 – Locations of Places. Use the pictures to introduce and drill the vocabulary words: mall, super market, hospital, drug store, and the preposition on the corner.

2. Demonstrate 'on the corner' by pantomime creating 'corners' and streets in the room using chairs and/or tables.

UNIT 2 – THE COMMUNITY
LESSON 1 – LOCATIONS OF PLACES

drug store

super market

on the corner of

hospital

mall

UNIT 2 – THE COMMUNITY - LESSON 1 – LOCATIONS OF PLACES
STUDENT BOOK PAGE 19

A. Drill Street Names
Use a Repetition Drill to introduce the Street Names on the map in the book .
Alternately, change the street names to streets in the community around your class'
location.

Go on to the next page and complete Time to Speak Conversation and Substitutions.
Return here later when prompted for the Let's Practice 2. Map Statements Listening
Activity with the map below:

B. Map Statements Listening Activity
1. Have students return to the map page.
2. Have students number a piece of paper 1-6.
3. Make the following true/false statements about the map. If your statement is
   true, have students write True on their papers. If your statement is NOT correct,
   have students write False on their papers.
4. Demonstrate by drawing two columns on the board labeled True and False:

	True	False
1.	x	
2.		
3.		

   [Continue to 6.]

5. Say the first statement: "The drug store is on the corner of Pines Boulevard and
   Douglas Road." Repeat 3 times. Students look at their maps and decide if the
   statement is True or False. Students mark No. 1 under the True column.

6. Use these statements:
   1. The drug store is on the corner of Pines Boulevard and Douglas Road. **[true]**
   2. The supermarket is on the corner of Johnson Street and Palm Avenue. **[true]**
   3. The mall is on the corner of Pines Boulevard and University Drive. **[false]**
   4. The hospital is on the corner of Sheridan Street and University Drive. **[true]**
   5. The mall is on the corner of Palm Avenue and Johnson Street. **[false]**
   6. The drug store is on the corner of Douglas Road and Palm Avenue. **[false]**

7. Go over student responses.

Return to the Let's Practice Activity 3. Play Beat the Cat.

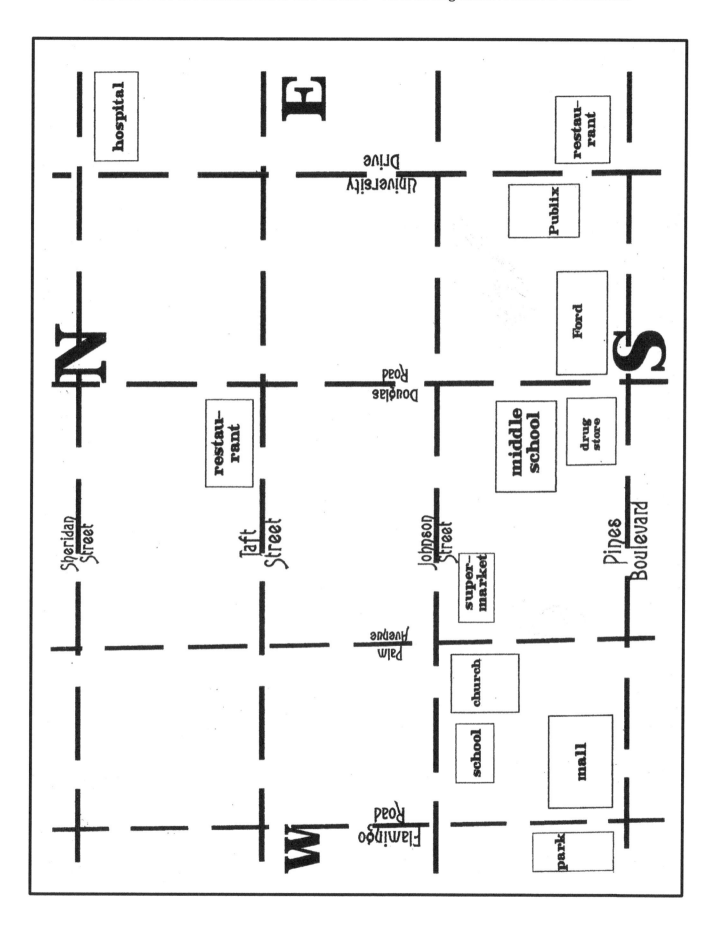

UNIT 2 – THE COMMUNITY - LESSON 1 – LOCATIONS OF PLACES
STUDENT BOOK PAGE 20

<u>Time to Speak</u>

A. Complete *To Do First*:
1. Introduce the conversation under Time to Speak. Have students repeat each line after the instructor. Repeat each line 5-6 times. Strive for a normal, conversational tone rather than an oral reading tone.
2. Use backward build up for sentences longer than 4 words. Remember to divide sentences into their sound units.
3. Use Intonation patterns including WH-Question and Statement.

B. Have students complete *To Do Second* and *To Do Third*.
Call on individual students to read the conversation after each substitution has been drilled.

Time to Speak

To Do First: Repeat the conversation after the instructor.

1.A. Excuse me. Where's **the mall?**
    1.B. **Pembroke Lakes Mall** is **on** **Pines Boulevard.**
2.A. **On Pines Boulevard?**
    2.B. Yes. **It's on the corner of** **Pines Boulevard and Flamingo Road.**
3.A. Thanks.

To Do Second: Speak with a partner. Change the <u>underlined words</u> in the conversation for the Substitutions in No. 1-3 below.

Substitution No. 1.
1.A. Excuse me. Where's the **drug store**?
    1.B. **Walgreens Drug Store is on Douglas Road**.
2.A. On **Douglas Road**?
    2.B. Yes. It's on the corner of **Douglas Road** and **Pines Boulevard**.
3.A. Thanks.

Substitution No. 2.
1.A. Excuse me. Where's the **hospital**?
    1.B. **Memorial Hospital Pembroke Pines is on Sheridan Street.**
2.A. On **Sheridan Street**?
    2.B. Yes. It's on the corner of **Sheridan Street** and **University Drive**.
3.A. Thanks.

Substitution No. 3.
1.A. Excuse me. Where's the **supermarket?**
    1.B. **Winn Dixie Supermarket is on Palm Avenue**.
2.A. On **Palm Avenue**?
    2.B. It's on the corner of **Palm Avenue** and **Johnson Street**.
3.A. Thanks.

To Do Third: Change partners and do Substitutions 1-3 again.

UNIT 2 – THE COMMUNITY - LESSON 1 – LOCATIONS OF PLACES
STUDENT BOOK PAGE 21

Practicing Perfect Pronunciation

Lead students in practicing pronouncing the contraction where's

Grammar Foundation

A. Introduce the Grammar Foundation by reading information under Prepositions of Location.

B. Complete *To Do First* by having students repeat each statement after the instructor. Repeat each one 5-6 times. After every 3 statements review.

C. Complete *To Do Second*. Demonstrate. Place a book on the table. Prompt students to make a statement about the book with a Preposition of Location, "The book is on the table." Continue placing the book in various locations to practice the prepositions of location introduced: on, next to, across from, and in.

D. Have students complete *To Do Third*.

~~*Practice Perfect Pronunciation*~~

In the question 'Where Is...' speakers contract the two words 'where is' into one word, the Contraction, WHERE'S. An apostrophe (') is used to show were letters have been dropped from the contraction. Practice pronouncing the contraction after the instructor.

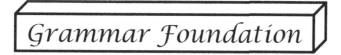

Prepositions of Location

Prepositions of Location are used to show the relationship of two objects to each other. Some common Prepositions of Location are: in, at, under, above, on, next to, between, across from, on the corner of. Here's the structure:

To Do First: Repeat each statement after the instructor.

Noun	+ Be +	Preposition +	Noun
The hospital	is	on	Sheridan Street.
The bank	is	next to	the post office.
The church	is	across from	the supermarket.
The sofa	is	in	the living room.
The book	is	on	the table.
My money	is	in	my purse.
The drug store is		on the corner of Douglas Road and Pines Boulevard.	

To Do Second:
The instructor will place a book somewhere, for example, on the table.
Students make a statement about the book with a Preposition of Location, for example, "The book is on the table."

To Do Third:
1. Work with a partner. Use your book.
2. Student 1 places the book somewhere, for example, on the table.
3. Student 2 will make a statement about the book with the correct Preposition of Location, for example, "The book is on the table."
4. Student 2 places the book somewhere.
5. Student 1 makes a statement with the Preposition of Location.

UNIT 2 – THE COMMUNITY - LESSON 1 – LOCATIONS OF PLACES
STUDENT BOOK PAGE 22

Let's Practice

A. Conduct the Let's Practice Activity 1. Read a Map
1. Have students locate the street name on their maps starting with Sheridan Street at the top.
2. Demonstrate using a finger to trace the length of Sheridan Street.
3. Continue locating and tracing the length of all street names.
4. Point to the places on the map starting with the hospital in the upper right.
5. Have students locate all the places as you name them on their maps.
6. Make statements taught earlier: "The hospital is on the corner of Sheridan Street and University Drive."
7. Ask students to make statements with each place name on the map.
8. Ask a question: "Where's the hospital?" Student answers: "The hospital is on the corner of Sheridan Street and University Drive."
9. Continue with questions and answers until all students have both asked and answered questions.

B. Conduct the Let's Practice Activity 2. Map Statements Listening
Turn back to the map page for teaching instructions.

C. Conduct the Let's Practice Activity 3. Beat the Cat
  See Activity Bank for instructions. Use the puzzle sentence: "Excuse me. Can I ask you a question? Where's the hospital?"

D. Conduct Let's Practice activity 4. Map Reading
1. Pair students.   Have students use the maps in their books.
2. Student pairs take turns asking questions about places on the map. For example:
Student 1: Where is the mall?
Student 2: The mall is on the corner of Pines Boulevard and Flamingo Road.

E. Conduct the Let's Practice Activity 5. Listening for Information
1. Ask: "Where is the Kingdom of God?" Listen for students' answers.
2. 2. Tell students: One day Jesus' disciples asked him when the Kingdom of God would begin. We can read what Jesus said to his disciples in the Bible in Luke 17:20-21.
3. Tell students: "Listen while I read Jesus' answer to this question: "Where is the kingdom of God?" Write the question on the board.
4. Read the passage 3 times: Jesus said to his disciples: "The Kingdom of God does not come in a way that you can see it. No one will say, 'Look, here it is!' or, "There it is!'; because the Kingdom of God is within you."
5. Ask students: "Where is the Kingdom of God?" [it is within us].
6. Write the scripture on the board "The Kingdom of God is within you."
7. Have students read it three times.

1. Read a Map

To Do: Open your book to your map. Follow the instructor's directions.

2. Map Statements Listening

1. Open your book to your map.
2. Number a piece of paper 1-6.
3. The instructor will make a statement about the map. For example: The drug store is on the corner of Pines Boulevard and Douglas Road.
4. Look at your map. If the statement is correct, write 'True' on your paper. If the statement is NOT correct, write 'False' on your paper.

3. Play Beat the Cat

1. This game is like the TV show Wheel of Fortune. The instructor will put a puzzle on the board.
2. Students take turns guessing consonants.
3. If the consonant is in the puzzle, the instructor will write it on the line. If the consonant is NOT in the puzzle, the instructor will draw part of a cat.
4. Continue until only vowels are left in the puzzle.

4. Map Reading

1. Work with a partner. Use your map.
2. Student 1 asks a question about the map, for example: 'Where's the mall?'
3. Student 2 answers the question, for example: 'The mall is on the corner of Pines Boulevard and Flamingo Road.'
4. Student 2 asks a question about the map.
5. Student 1 answers the question.

5. Listening for Information

1. The instructor will write a question on the board.
2. The instructor will read a passage. Listen for the answer to the question.

Jesus said to his disciples: "The Kingdom of God does not come in a way that you can see it. No one will say, 'Look, here it is!' or, "There it is!'; because the Kingdom of God is within you."

UNIT 2 – THE COMMUNITY - LESSON 1 – LOCATIONS OF PLACES
STUDENT BOOK PAGE 23

<u>Review Exercises</u>

1. <u>Hidden Word Puzzle</u>
Circle the words in the puzzle.

Answer Key – words in bold

CHURCH   DRUG STORE   HOSPITAL
SUPERMARKET   SCHOOL   MALL

```
Q W E R P A R K T R J K L N M E W B C X
I J H N M K L P O I U S C H O O L K H Y
F D S A J H O S P I T A L E Q W R N M C
C C H U R C H H H I O U N L E W C H K W
J I W A C R O S S F R O M K L J N B D G
K J E O I N K O I U E U O O J M A L L K
J K I J E R T W Q S D F N E X T T O J W
K N B D R U G S T O R E N D S S D G E X
N K L S U P E R M A R K E T H N B V G D
```

2. <u>Scrambled Spelling</u>
Spell the street names correctly.

Answer Key -

1. eniiurtvsy rvdie   *University Drive*

2. hiadesrn tetsre   *Sheridan Street*

3. alpm uvaene   *Palm Avenue*

4. lmanoifg ador   *Flamingo Road*

5. iesnp uoblvread   *Pines Boulevard*

6. ojnhosn tertse   *Johnson Street*

Review Exercises

1. Hidden Word Puzzle

Circle the words in the puzzle.

| CHURCH | DRUG STORE | HOSPITAL | SUPERMARKET | SCHOOL |
| MALL | | | | |

```
Q  W  E  L  R  [P  A  R  K]  T  R  J  K  L  N  M  E  W  B  C  X
I  J  H  X  N  M  K  L  P  O  I  U  S  C  H  O  O  L  K  H  Y
F  D  S  A  J  H  O  S  P  I  T  A  L  E  Q  W  R  N  M  C  W
C  C  H  U  R  C  H  H  I  O  U  N  L  E  W  C  H  K  W  M
J  I  W  A  C  R  O  S  S  F  R  O  M  K  L  J  N  B  D  G  O
K  J  E  O  I  N  K  O  I  U  E  U  O  O  J  M  A  L  L  K  D
J  K  I  J  E  R  T  W  Q  S  D  F  N  E  X  T  T  O  J  W  A
K  N  B  D  R  U  G  S  T  O  R  E  N  D  S  S  D  G  E  X  Z
N  K  L  S  U  P  E  R  M  A  R  K  E  T  H  N  B  V  G  D  J
```

2. Scrambled Spelling

Unscramble the words. Spell the street names correctly. Write the names on the lines.

1. eniiurtvsy rvdie   ***University Drive*** _____

2. hiadesrn tetsre _____

3. alpm uvaene _____

4. lmanoifg ador _____

5. iesnp uoblvread _____

6. ojnhosn tertse _____

UNIT 2 – THE COMMUNITY - LESSON 2 – EMERGENCIES
STUDENT BOOK PAGE 24

A. Prayer for Students & Self

B. Lesson Objective and Functions:
- Reporting emergencies to proper authorities
- Giving personal information : Name, Address, Phone Number

C. Grammar Structures:
- Present Progressive Tense

D. Biblical Reference or Principles:
- When we are afraid we can remember that God siad in Hebrews 13:5-6: "Never will I leave you; never will I forsake you. So we say with confidence, "The Lord is my helper; I will not be afraid. What can man do to me?"

E. Materials & Preparation:
- Prepare a Concentration Game Board. See directions in Activity Bank
- Prepare Concentration Game cards. Print the following matches on individual 4x6 index cards:

Is this an emergency?	Yes!
What's your name?	John Smith.
What's your address?	4801 North Park Road, Hollywood
What's your phone number?	954.435.8800

Introduction
1. Ask students if they have ever had any emergency situations. Ask what they did.
2. If no student has a story, you may try pantomiming an emergency among the instructors such as one instructor is choking, another teacher calls 911, and the third instructor is the 911 operator who gives directions to handle the emergency.
3. Tell students they are going to learn how to call the 911 operator today for emergencies.

UNIT 2 – THE COMMUNITY
LESSON 2 – EMERGENCIES

For emergencies call 911

UNIT 2 – THE COMMUNITY - LESSON 2 – EMERGENCIES
STUDENT BOOK PAGE 25

<u>Introduce New Vocabulary</u>
1. Have students open to Unit 2 – The Community; Lesson 2 – Emergencies.
2. Introduce the vocabulary words: police, ambulance, broken leg, burglar, and fire.
3. Use the words: broken leg, burglar, and fire in the sentences as under each picture.
4. Drill the sentences using backward build up. Remember to divide sentences into their sound units.
5. Demonstrate excitement in the voice, for example: "My mother broke her leg!!!" and a whispering voice for, "There's a burglar in my house!!"

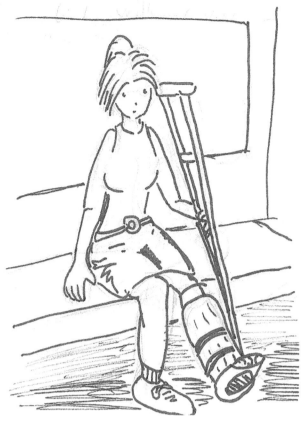

my mother broke her leg

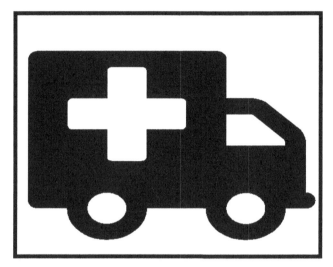

ambulance

there's a burglar
in my house

my house is on fire

UNIT 2 – THE COMMUNITY - LESSON 2 – EMERGENCIES
STUDENT BOOK PAGE 26

Time to Speak

A. Complete *To Do First:*
   1. Introduce the conversation under Time to Speak. Have students repeat each line after the instructor. Repeat each line 5-6 times. Strive for a normal, conversational tone rather than an oral reading tone.
   2. Use backward build up for sentences longer than 4 words. Remember to divide sentences into their sound units.
   3. Use correct intonation, stress, and rhythm patterns. Include the following intonation patterns:
   - Yes/No Question Intonation: Raise the voice steadily up to the last word before the question mark.
   - Statement
   - WH-Question.
Remember to use excitement in the voice reflecting the content of the conversation.

B. Introduce whispering for Substitution No. 1: There's a burglar in my house. Practice as a group.

C. Have students complete *To Do Second.*

D. Student pairs present their conversations and substitutions to the class.

Calling 911 Emergency!

1.A.   911. Is this an emergency?
    1.B.   Yes! **My mother broke her leg**.
2.A.   **The ambulance is** coming. What's your name?
    2.B.   **Kathy Johnson**.
3A.   What's your address?
    3.B.   **50 Madrid Lane, Davie**
4.A.   What's your phone number?
    4.B.   **954.274.3105.**
5.A.   **The ambulance is** coming.
    5.B.   Thank you.

To Do First:
Repeat the conversation after the instructor.
To Do Second:
Speak with a partner. Change the underlined words in the conversation for the Substitutions.

Substitution No. 1

1.A.   911. Is this an emergency?
    1.B.   **There's a burglar in my house**!
2.A.   **The police** are coming. What's your name?
    2.B.   **Robin Francois.**
3.A.   What's your address?
    3.B.   **15427 N.W. 13 Street, Pembroke Pines.**
4.A.   What's your phone number?
    4.B.   **954.430.2387**.
5.A.   The police are coming.
    5.B.   Thank you.

Substitution No. 2

1.A.   911. Is this an emergency?
    1.B.   **There's a fire in my house**!
2.A.   **The fire department** is coming. What's your name?
    2.B.   **Juan Diaz**.
3.A.   What's your address?
    3.B.   **5140 S.W. 90 Avenue, Cooper City**.
4.A.   What's your phone number?
    4.B.   **954.436.9289**.
5.A.   **The fire department** is coming.
    5.B.   Thank you.

UNIT 2 – THE COMMUNITY - LESSON 2 – EMERGENCIES
STUDENT BOOK PAGE 27

Practicing Perfect Pronunciation

Pronouncing Phone Numbers
Demonstrate pronunciation of phone numbers as shown in student text.
Repeat all the phone numbers in the conversation.

Grammar Foundation
Present Progressive Tense

A. Introduce the Grammar Foundation by reading information under Present Progressive Tense.

B. Complete *To Do* by having students repeat the example sentences after the instructor. Be sure to use the Statement intonation pattern.

~~ *Practicing Perfect Pronunciation* ~~

Pronouncing Phone Numbers

English speakers pronounce phone numbers as follows:

954   274   31   05

This pronunciation is easy to understand because English speakers are expecting to hear phone numbers pronounced in this way.

To Do:

Repeat each phone number after the instructor. Use the pronunciation pattern above.

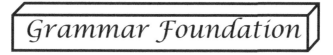

Present Progressive Tense

Also known as Present Continuous Tense, we use the Present Progressive Tense to describe action that is happening at the present moment. It is continuous action. It is action that is happening while the speaker is speaking. Here's the grammar structure:

To Do: Repeat the sentences after the instructor.

Affirmative Statements

Subject + Be Verb + Main Verb + 'Ing Ending

Singular Forms

I	am	call	ing	911.
You	are	talk	ing	to the police.
He	is	send	ing	an ambulance.
She	is	tak	ing	a shower.
The house is		burn	ing.	

Plural Forms

We	are	do	ing	exercise.
We	are	study	ing.	
They	are	read	ing	their books.

UNIT 2 – THE COMMUNITY - LESSON 2 – EMERGENCIES
STUDENT BOOK PAGE 28

Let's Practice

A. Conduct the Let's Practice Activity 1. Play 911 Operator Concentration
   1. See Activity Bank for directions to prepare a Concentration Game Board and for how to play Concentration.
   2. Prepare Concentration cards using the questions and answers from the dialogue:

Is this an emergency?	Yes!
What's your name?	John Smith.
What's your address?	4801 North Park Road, Hollywood
What's your phone number?	954.435.8800

B. Conduct the Let's Practice Activity 2. Dictation – Addresses and Phone Numbers
   1. Have students open their books to the Dictation activity.
   2. Dictate both addresses and phone numbers from the conversation and the substitutions.
   3. Repeat as often as students request.
   4. Go over student responses.

C. Conduct the Let's Practice Activity 3. Emergency Role Play
   1. Pair students.
   2. Assign one of the Emergency Role Play scenarios in the boxes to each pair.
   3. Give a few minutes to rehearse or prepare their role plays.
   4. Pairs present their role plays to the class.

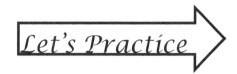

Let's Practice

1. Play 911 Operator Concentration

1. Work with a partner or work with the whole class.

2. In the Concentration board are 8 cards. Four cards have 911 operator questions and 4 cards have answers.

3. Student 1 chooses 2 cards from the Concentration board and reads them to the class. For example: a question and the correct answer. If the 2 cards match – they are removed from the board and Student 1 receives one point.

4. Student 2 chooses 2 cards and reads them to the class. If these 2 cards do NOT match – Student 2 puts these cards back into the board.

5. Continue until all cards are matched and removed from the board.

2. Dictation – Addresses and Phone Numbers
The instructor will dictate some addresses and phone numbers. Write them below.

Addresses   Phone Numbers

1. _____

2. _____

3. _____

3. Emergency Role Play
Work with a partner. Student 1 is the 911 Operator. Student 2 is the caller with the emergency.

1. You saw two cars in an accident on I-95. A woman is hurt. Call 911.

2. Your neighbor is not home. Someone is breaking into his window.

3. Your husband fell off the ladder and he can't move. Call 911.

UNIT 2 – THE COMMUNITY - LESSON 2 – EMERGENCIES
STUDENT BOOK PAGE 29

D. Conduct the Let's Practice Activity 4. Play Beat the Cat
NOTE: This activity is the biblical principle, Hebrews 13:6 The Lord is my helper; I will not be afraid.
See Activity Bank for directions how to prepare the puzzle and how to play the game.
After students solve the puzzle, consider commenting on the verse.

Review Exercises

Review Exercises are intended to be assigned for homework. Be sure students understand how to complete each exercise.

1. Complete the Conversation
Answer Key – answers in bold

1.A. 911. Is this an **emergency** / address?

1.B. Yes! My daughter **broke** / drank her arm.

2.A. An **ambulance** / fire department is on the way. What's your address / **name** ?

2.A. Kathy Smith.

3.A. What's your phone number / **address?**

3.A. 11734 S.W. 55 Street, Cooper City.

4.A. What's your name / **phone number**?

4.B. 954.434.1101.

2. Write Answers to the Questions
Answer Key – in bold

1. Is this an emergency? *Yes!* _____

2. What's your name? **student's name** _____

3. What's your address? **student's address** _____

4. What's your phone number? **student's phone** _____

4. Play Beat the Cat

1. This game is like the TV show Wheel of Fortune. The instructor will put a puzzle on the board.

2. Students take turns guessing consonants.

3. If the consonant is in the puzzle, the instructor will write it on the line. If the consonant is NOT in the puzzle, the instructor will draw part of a cat.

4. Continue until only vowels are left in the puzzle.

Review Exercises

1. Complete the Conversation. Circle the Correct Word

1.A.   911. Is this an emergency / address?

   1.B.   Yes! My daughter broke / drank her arm.

2.A.   An ambulance / fire department is coming. What's your address / name ?

   2.A.   Kathy Smith.

3.A.   What's your   phone number / address?

   3.A.   11734 S.W. 55 Street, Cooper City.

4.A.   What's your name / phone number?

   4.B.   954.434.1101.

2. Write Answers to the Questions

1. Is this an emergency? *Yes!* _____

2. What's your name?   _____

3. What's your address?   _____

4. What's your phone number?   _____

UNIT 2 – THE COMMUNITY - LESSON 2 – EMERGENCIES
STUDENT BOOK PAGE 30

3. Spell the Words Correctly
Answer Key – in bold

1. s d a e d r s   *address*

2. p o e h n m u n e b r   **phone number**

3. n g e e m c e y r   **emergency**

4. Complete the Sentences. Use the Present Progressive Tense and the Verbs in Parentheses
Answer Key – in bold

Example: (walk) John **is walking** to work right now.

1. (send) The 911 Operator **is sending** an ambulance now.

2. (call) The woman **is calling** 911 Emergency.

3. (watch) I **am watching** TV now.

4. (drink) They **are drinking** Coca Cola now.

5. (send) The 911 Operator **is sending** the police.

6. (tell) The man **is telling** the 911 Operator his address.

7. (call) My mother and father **are calling** the 911 Operator.

8. (send) The 911 Operator **is sending** an ambulance.

9. (put) The firemen **are putting** out the fire.

10. (take) The burglar **is taking** my neighbor's TV.

3. Spell the Words Correctly

1. s d a e d r s   ***address*** _____

2. p o e h n m u n e b r   _____

3. n g e e m c e y r   _____

4. Complete the Sentences. Use the Present Progressive Tense and the Verbs in Parentheses

Example: (walk) John ***is walking*** to work right now.

1. (send) The 911 Operator _____ an ambulance now.

2. (call) The woman _____ 911 Emergency.

3. (watch) I _____ TV now.

4. (drink) They _____ Coca Cola now.

5. (send) The 911 Operator _____ the police.

6. (tell) The man _____ the 911 Operator his address.

7. (call) My mother and father _____ the 911 Operator.

8. (send) The 911 Operator _____ an ambulance.

9. (put) The firemen _____ out the fire.

10. (take) The burglar _____ my neighbor's TV.

UNIT 3 – LET'S EAT - LESSON 1 – SUPERMARKET DEPARTMENTS
STUDENT BOOK PAGE 31

A. Prayer for Students & Self

B. Lesson Objective and Functions:
- Categorizing foods into departments of the supermarket
- Requesting location of foods in various departments of the supermarket

C. Grammar Structures:
- Contractions: Pronoun + Will; Pronoun + Be

D. Biblical Reference or Principles:
- Matthew 6:11 - Give us today our daily bread

E. Materials & Preparation:
- For Check Your Senses activity: styrofoam cups; tin foil to cover styrofoam cups; rubber bands to secure tin foil; sandwich sized brown paper bags; prepare supermarket department name "tents" from card stock by folding 8 ½ x 11" paper into thirds and tape so they stand up.
- Food items or products, one each, placed into sandwich sized brown paper bags: potato, apple, lettuce, tomato, orange, and paper towel. Number the bags with a marker.
- Food items, place a small portion, one each, into styrofoam cups: cupcake, peanut butter, milk, cheesecake, butter, and a slice of turkey lunchmeat. Cover each with tinfoil secured with rubber band, and number the cups.
- Prepare a chart of Matthew 6:11 - Give us today our daily bread. Alternately, write on boad.

Introduction
1. Ask: Who likes to go to the supermarket?
2. Which supermarket do you shop at? [write supermarket names on board]
3. What is one thing you buy at the supermarket? [get student responses]
4. Say: "Tonight we are going to learn how foods are divided into departments in the supermarket."

Introduce New Vocabulary
1. Have students open to Unit 3 – Let's Eat; Lesson 1 – Supermarket Departments.
2. Introduce the 5 supermarket departments using a repetition drill.
3. For each department, ask: "What foods would you find in this department?"

UNIT 3 – LET'S EAT
LESSON 1 - SUPERMARKET DEPARTMENTS

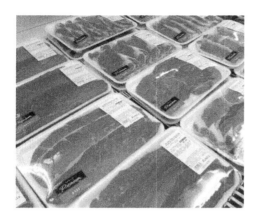

Meat Department

Grocery Department

Bakery Department

Dairy Department

Produce Department

UNIT 3 – LET'S EAT - LESSON 1 – SUPERMARKET DEPARTMENTS
STUDENT BOOK PAGE 32

1. Introduce each food word using a repetition drill. Repeat each word 5-6 times.
2. Ask students about each item:
   - Who likes this?
   - Who doesn't like this?
   - Who eats this?
   - How often do you eat this?
   - Ask other questions as desired.
3. After each is introduced, list on the board.
4. Spell each word. Have students repeat. For interest, use a rhythm like a chant.

ground beef

orange

cupcake

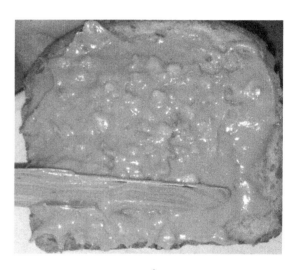

peanut butter

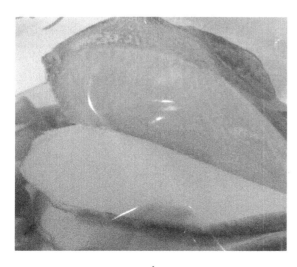

turkey

milk

UNIT 3 – LET'S EAT - LESSON 1 – SUPERMARKET DEPARTMENTS
STUDENT BOOK PAGE 33

Continue introducing Vocabulary:

1. Introduce each food word using a repetition drill.   Repeat each word 5-6 times.
2. Ask students about each item:
   - Who likes this?
   - Who doesn't like this?
   - Who eats this?
   - How often do you eat this?
3. Ask other questions as desired.
4. After each is introduced, list on the board.
5. Spell each word. Have students repeat. For interest, use a rhythm like a chant.

tomatoes

lettuce

cheese cake

butter

potatoes

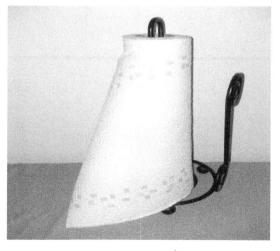

paper towels

UNIT 3 – LET'S EAT - LESSON 1 – SUPERMARKET DEPARTMENTS
STUDENT BOOK PAGE 34

Time to Speak

A. Complete *To Do First:*

1. Introduce the conversation under Time to Speak. Have students repeat each line after the instructor. Repeat each line 5-6 times. Strive for a normal, conversation tone rather than an oral reading tone.

2. Use backward build up for sentences longer than 4 words. Remember to divide sentences into their sound units.

3. Use correct intonation, stress, and rhythm patterns. Include the following intonation patterns:

- WH-Question intonation
- AND intonation as in 'milk and butter'
- Statement

B. Have students complete *To Do Second and To Do Third.* Call on individual students to read the conversation after each substitution has been drilled.

Time to Speak

To Do First: Repeat the conversation after the instructor.

Shopping in the Supermarket

1.A.   What's on the shopping list today?

   1.B.   We need **milk and butter.**

2.A. They're in the **Dairy Department.**

   2.B.   We also need **ground beef and turkey.**

3.A.   They're in the **Meat Department.**

   3.B.   Good. We'll finish shopping quickly.

To Do Second: Speak with a partner. Change the underlined words in the conversation for the Substitutions in No. 1 and No. 2. below.

Substitution No. 1

   1.B.   oranges and potatoes

2.A.   Produce Department

   2.B.   paper towels and peanut butter

3.A.   Grocery Department

Substitution No. 2

   1.B.   lettuce and tomatoes

2.A.   Produce Department

   2.B.   cheesecake and cupcakes

3.A.   Bakery Department

To Do Third: Change partners and repeat Substitutions No. 1 and No. 2 again.

UNIT 3 – LETS EAT - LESSON 1 – SUPERMARKET DEPARTMENTS
STUDENT BOOK PAGE 35

Grammar Foundation

A. Introduce the Grammar Foundation by reading information under Contractions.

B. Complete _To Do First_ by having students repeat each contraction after the instructor. Repeat each one 5-6 times. After each set, review.

C. Complete _To Do Second_ by using a koosh ball or other soft object or even a wadded piece of paper. Throw the ball to one student while you say one of the two words, for example, "I will". Student catches the ball and responds with the contraction, for example, "I'll". Student then throws the ball back to the instructor. Continue tossing the ball randomly until all students have participated several times.

D. Have students complete _To Do Third._ Circulate to ensure students understand task and are completing it correctly.

Grammar Foundation

Contractions

English speakers use Contractions which are two words put together to form another shorter word. Some letters are left out of one of the words and an apostrophe ['] marks the place where the letters are left out.

To Do First: Repeat each contraction after the instructor.

Subject + Will = Contraction			Subject + Be = Contraction		
I	will	I'll	I	am	I'm
you	will	you'll	you	are	you're
he	will	he'll	he	is	he's
she	will	she'll	she	is	she's
it	will	it'll	it	is	it's
we	will	we'll	we	are	we're
they	will	they'll	they	are	they're

To Do Second:
1. The instructor will say the two words, for example, "I am".
2. The instructor will throw a ball to a student.
3. The student catches the ball.
4. The student says the contraction, for example, "I'm".
5. The student throws the ball to the instructor.

To Do Third:
1. Work with a partner.
2. Student 1 says the two words.
3. Student 2 says the Contraction.
4. Student 2 says the 2 words.
5. Student 1 says the Contraction.

To Do Fourth:
1. Work with a partner.
2. Take turns saying sentences with Contractions and the Vocabulary words.
3. Say your sentences for the class.

UNIT 3 – LETS EAT - LESSON 1 – SUPERMARKET DEPARTMENTS
STUDENT BOOK PAGE 36

Let's Practice

A. Conduct the Let's Practice Activity 1. Check Your Senses.
   1. Prepare the activity in advance. Materials: styrofoam cups; tin foil to cover styrofoam cups; rubber bands to secure tin foil; sandwich sized brown paper bags.
   2. Food items or products, one each, placed into sandwich sized brown paper bags: potato, apple, lettuce, tomato, orange, and paper towel. Number the outside of each bag with a marker.
   3. Food items, place a small portion, one each, into styrofoam cups: cupcake, peanut butter, milk, cheesecake, butter, and a slice of turkey lunchmeat. Cover each with tinfoil secured with rubber band, and number the outside of each cup. Punch a few small holes in the top of the tin foil enough to let the smell of the item escape, but not large enough to see the contents inside.
   4. Place the filled styrofoam cups on one table in the room and the filled paper bags on another table. If available, have a teacher monitor each of the tables.
   5. Have students turn in their books to the Check Your Senses activity. Give instructions. Students guess what is inside each bag by feeling the contents with their hand only without looking into the bag. Students guess what is inside each cup by smelling the contents through the punched holes without looking inside or removing the tinfoil cover.
   6. Students write their responses in their books.
   7. Go over students' responses.   Reveal the bag and cup contents so students can check their correct/incorrect responses.

B. Have students complete the Let's Practice Activity 2. Search the Supermarket.
   1. Collect their pictures and place them on a table.
   2. Prepare in advance supermarket department name "tents" from card stock by folding an 8 ½ x 11" paper into thirds and tape together so they stand up. Place the department tents around the room creating the supermarket departments.
   3. Students take the pictures from the table and distribute them into the departments.
   4. To check work, have students report what's in each department.

C. Have students complete the Let's Practice Activity 3. Supermarket Shopping.
   1. Collect students' papers, aka, shopping lists. Redistribute one list to each student.
   2. Students 'shop' for their list picking up the pictures of each item which were distributed into the departments in the Search the Supermarket activity.

D. Have students complete the Let's Practice Activity 4. Food Vocabulary Expansion.
   Divide students into small groups. Assign one supermarket department to each group. Students work together to list foods that are found in that department. Consider allowing the use of dictionaries, phones, or tablets. When finished, students share their lists with the class.

1. Check Your Senses

1. Smell each cup. Write what you think is inside.
2. Feel inside each bag. Write what you think is inside.

Cup 1 _____   Bag 1 _____

Cup 2 _____   Bag 2 _____

Cup 3 _____   Bag 3 _____

Cup 4 _____   Bag 4 _____

Cup 5 _____   Bag 5 _____

Cup 6 _____   Bag 6 _____

2. Search the Supermarket

1. Draw a picture of one of the food words on a piece of paper, for example, draw an orange.
2. Draw two more pictures of different foods. Give your pictures to the instructor.

3. Supermarket Shopping

1. On a piece of paper, write 5 of the food words.
2. Give your paper to the instructor.

4. Food Vocabulary Expansion

1. Work with a small group. The instructor will give your group one of the supermarket departments, for example, the Meat Department.
2. With your group, write a list of foods you can find in your department. You can use your dictionary or your phone or tablet.
3. Share your list with the class.

UNIT 3 – LET'S EAT - LESSON 1 – SUPERMARKET DEPARTMENTS
STUDENT BOOK PAGE 37

E. Have students complete the Let's Practice Activity 5. What Do You Like?
They can stay in the same small groups, or regroup. Students report to the class what their group members said.

F. Complete the Let's Practice Activity 6. Practice English Rhythm
  Note this is the biblical principle.
1. Prepare in advance a chart with the verse Matthew 6:11: Give us today our daily bread. Alternately, write on the board.
2. Repeat the verse, clapping an even rhythm. Remember the sound units and clap on the content words: give, today, daily, bread.
3. Share any thoughts about the verse.

Review Exercises

Assign Review Exercises for homework

1. Alphabetize activity. Be sure students understand alphabetical order. Refer to the example words: butter and cheesecake.

Answer Key – in bold

butter, cheesecake, cup cakes, ground beef, lettuce, milk, oranges, paper towels, peanut butter, potatoes, tomatoes, turkey.

5. What Do You Like?

1. Talk with a small group.
2. Tell your group which foods you like to eat. Which foods do you not like to eat. What is your favorite food?

6. Practice English Rhythm

Jesus taught his disciples to pray to God and ask Him to give them food every day. Here's what Jesus told his disciples to pray:

Give us today our daily bread.

To Do:
Repeat the sentence after the instructor 7 times.

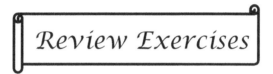

Review Exercises

1. Alphabetize

Put the food words into alphabetical (A-Z) order.

milk	butter	ground beef	turkey	oranges	potatoes
tomatoes	lettuce	peanut butter	cheesecake	cup cakes	paper towels

___**butter, cheesecake**_____

_____

_____

_____

_____

_____

UNIT 3 – LET'S EAT - LESSON 1 – SUPERMARKET DEPARTMENTS
STUDENT BOOK PAGE 38

2. Categorize.
Answer Key – in bold

Dairy	Meat	Produce	Grocery	Bakery
butter	**ground beef**	**lettuce**	**paper towels**	**cheesecake**
milk	**turkey**	**oranges**	**peanut butter**	**cup cakes**
		potatoes		
		tomatoes		

4. Match the Full Form with the Contraction
Write the letter on the line by the Full Form.
Answer Key – in bold

	Full Form	Contraction
d.	I will	a. you're
k.	you will	b. she's
e.	he will	c. we're
l.	she will	d. I'll
f.	it will	e. he'll
m.	we will	f. it'll
g.	they will	g. they'll
n.	I am	h. he's
a.	you are	i. it's
h.	he is	j. they're
b.	she is	k. you'll
i.	it is	l. she'll
c.	we are	m. we'll
j.	they are	n. I'm

2. Categorize
Put the food words into the Supermarket Departments.

Dairy	Meat	Produce	Grocery	Bakery
Butter				**cheesecake**

3. At Home
Look in your kitchen. Write a list of 10 foods you have. Bring your list to the next class.

4. Matching

Match the Full Form with the Contraction. Write the letter on the line by the Full Form.

	Full Form	Contraction
d.	I will	a. you're
	you will	b. she's
	he will	c. we're
	she will	d. I'll
	it will	e. he'll
	we will	f. it'll
	they will	g. they'll
	I am	h. he's
	you are	i. it's
	he is	j. they're
	she is	k. you'll
	it is	l. she'll
	we are	m. we'll
	they are	n. I'm

UNIT 3 – LET'S EAT - LESSON 2 – FOOD PACKAGING AND MEASUREMENTS
STUDENT BOOK PAGE 39

A. Prayer for Students & Self

B. Lesson Objective and Functions:
- Describing basic food packaging and measurements of food products in the supermrket
- Listing food products needed at the supermarket

C. Grammar Structures:
- Count and Noncount Nouns
- Using There is; There are; There isn't; and There aren't
- Using Some and Any

D. Biblical Reference or Principles:
- Matthew 4:4 – Jesus said, "It is written: 'Man does not live on bread alone, but on every word that comes from the mouth of God.'"

E. Materials & Preparation:
- Make food word cards for There's a Carton of Juice in the Refrigerator Activity
- Tacky tape or blue painter's tape to affix cards to the board
- Shopping List to post outside of the room for Shopping List Activity
- 2 Sets of Scrambled Sentence cards Matthew 4:4

Introduction
Say: "I went to the supermarket this week and I bought …" [name 2-3 items]. "What did you buy?"
Ask: "Who went to the supermarket this week? What did you buy?" [get student responses]
Say: "Tonight we are going to learn some food words in English."

Introduce New Vocabulary
Have students open to Unit 3 – Let's Eat; Lesson 2 – Food Packaging and Measurements. Introduce the storage places including: refrigerator, freezer, and kitchen cabinet using a Repetition Drill.

UNIT 3 – LET'S EAT
LESSON 2 – FOOD PACKAGING AND MEASUREMENTS

refrigerator

freezer

kitchen cabinet

UNIT 3 – LET'S EAT - LESSON 2 – FOOD PACKAGING AND MEASUREMENTS
STUDENT BOOK PAGE 40

1. Introduce each food word using a repetition drill.
2. Ask students about each item:
   - Who likes this?
   - Who doesn't like this?
   - Who eats this?
   - How often do you eat this?
   - Other questions as desired.
3. After each is introduced, list on the board.
4. Spell each word. Have students repeat. For interest, use a rhythm like a chant.

a carton of juice

a dozen eggs

a box of crackers

a can of soup

a gallon of ice cream

a package of meat

UNIT 3 – LET'S EAT - LESSON 2 – FOOD PACKAGING AND MEASUREMENTS
STUDENT BOOK PAGE 41

Time to Speak

A. Complete *To Do First:*

1. Introduce the conversation under Time to Speak. Have students repeat each line after the instructor. Repeat each line 5-6 times. Strive for a normal, conversation tone rather than an oral reading tone.
2. Use backward build up for sentences longer than 4 words. Remember to divide sentences into their sound units.
3. Use correct intonation, stress, and rhythm patterns. Include the following intonation patterns:

- Yes/No Question: the voice rises steadily until the last word before the question mark.
- Statement: the voice starts higher and moves downward like going down a staircase through each sound unit in a statement. When the end of the statement is reached, at the period, the voice falls.
- AND to Join Two Items: both items are said with equal stress while 'and' that joins them is said with a low tone.

B. Have students complete *To Do Second*. Call on individual students to read the conversation after each substitution has been drilled.

Is There Any More Juice?

To Do First: Repeat the conversation after the instructor.

1.A.   **Is there** any more **juice** in the **refrigerator**?
   1.B.   No, there **isn't**. We need to buy some more.
2.A.   What else do we need at the supermarket?
   2.B.   We need **a dozen eggs**.
3.A.   I'll make a list. O.K. that's **a carton of juice** and **a dozen eggs**.

To Do Second: Speak with a partner. Change the underlined words in the conversation for the Substitutions in No. 1-2 below.

Substitution No. 1

1.A.   **Are there** any more **crackers** in the **cabinet**?
   1.B.   No, there **aren't**.
2.A.   What else do we need at the supermarket?
   2.B.   We need **a can of soup**.
3.A.   I'll make a list. O.K. that's **a box of crackers** and **a can of soup**.

Substitution No. 2

1.A.   **Is there** any more **meat** in the **freezer**?
   1.B.   No, there **isn't**. We need to buy some more.
2.A.   What else do we need at the supermarket?
   2.B.   We need **a gallon of ice cream**.
3.A.   I'll make a list. O.K. that's **a package of meat** and **a gallon of ice cream**.

UNIT 3 – LET'S EAT - LESSON 2 – FOOD PACKAGING AND MEASUREMENTS
STUDENT BOOK PAGE 42

Grammar Foundation

A. Introduce the Grammar Foundation by reading information under Count and NonCount Nouns.

B. `Introduce the Grammar Foundation by reading the information under There is; There are; There isn't; There aren't.

C. Complete _To Do Second_ by having students repeat each example sentence after the instructor.

Grammar Foundation

To Do First: Read the information about Count and Noncount Nouns. Repeat the example statements after the instructor.

1. Count and Noncount Nouns

1. Count Nouns can be counted as individual items, for example: an apple, a carrot, the car. Count Nouns also have a plural form, for example: four apples, a pound of carrots, 20 cars. Use an Article in front of the Count Noun: A, An, The, Some or Any.

2. Noncount Nouns cannot be counted because they are very small pieces and cannot be counted, for example: sugar, rice. Noncount Nouns can also be liquids such as water or milk. Noncount Nouns do not have a plural form. Use Some or Any in front of Noncount Nouns.

3. Noncount Nouns can be counted when they are inside of packages, but you are counting the package, which is a Count Noun, for example: 2 gallons of milk, 6 cartons of juice, 4 bags of rice.

To Do Second: Read the information about making statements and questions with THERE. Repeat the example statements after the instructor.

2. There is; There are; There isn't; There aren't

1. Use THERE IS... for Affirmative Statements with Singular Count Nouns and Noncount Nouns. For example:
   - There is an apple on the table.   [singular count]
   - There is some juice in the refrigerator.   [noncount]

2. Use THERE ARE ... for Affirmative Statements with Plural Count Nouns.
   - There are some cookies in the cabinet.   [plural count]
   - There are some cars in the parking lot.   [plural count]

3. Use IS THERE ... ? for Questions with Singular Count Nouns and Noncount Nouns. For example:
   - Is there an apple on the table?   [singular count]   Yes, there is.
   - Is there any ice cream in the freezer?   [noncount]   No, there isn't.

4. Use ARE THERE ... ? for Questions with Plural Count Nouns. For example:
   - Are there any cookies in the cabinet?   [plural count]   Yes, there are.
   - Are there any apples on the table?   [plural count]   No, there aren't.

UNIT 3 – LET'S EAT - LESSON 2 – FOOD PACKAGING AND MEASUREMENTS
STUDENT BOOK PAGE 43

D. Introduce Some and Any with Count and Noncount nouns. Read the information.

E. Have students complete _To Do Third_ by repeating the example sentences after the instructor.

Practicing Perfect Pronunciation

Practice English Rhythm with the activity I'm Going to the Store to Buy Some Eggs – Add On Game.
1. Demonstrate the Add On Game.
2. Instructor begins by saying "I'm Going to the Store to Buy a dozen eggs."
3. Student 1 repeats the statement and then add another item to the shopping list, for example: "I'm going to the store to buy a dozen eggs and a carton of juice.
4. Student 2 repeats the statements and adds a new item. For example: "I'm going to the store to buy a dozen eggs, a carton of juice, and a package of meat."
5. Play continues around the room until all students have added a new food item. The goal is to practice the vocabulary learned in the lesson and add other items students may wish.

Let's Practice

Complete the Let's Practice Activity 1. Dictation
1. List the food words from the vocabulary on the board.
2. Dictate some measurements, for example: a box of...; a carton of...; a package of...
3. Students write what is dictated.
4. Students then complete their sentences using the appropriate food words from the board.
5. Students then read their sentences to the class.

To Do Third: Read the information about using Some and Any with Count and Noncount Nouns. Repeat the example statements after the instructor.

3. Some and Any

1. Use SOME to make Affirmative Statements and ask Questions with Plural Count Nouns and Noncount Nouns. For example:
- I have some apples. [plural count noun]
- We have some video games. [plural count noun]
- He has some juice. [noncount noun]
- They have some ice cream. [noncount noun]

2. Use ANY to make Negative Statements and ask Questions with both Count and Noncount Nouns. For example:
- He doesn't have any apples. [plural count] Does he have any apples?
- He doesn't have any juice. [noncount] Does he have any juice?
- We don't have any video games. [plural count] Do we have any video games?
- They don't have any ice cream. [noncount] Do they have any ice cream?

~~ *Practicing Perfect Pronunciation* ~~

I'm Going to the Store to Buy Some Eggs – Add On Game
1. The Instructor begins by saying, "I'm going to the store to buy some eggs."
2. Student 1 repeats the statement, "I'm going to the store to buy some eggs," and adds another item to the shopping list, for example: "I'm going to the store to buy some eggs and a carton of juice."
3. Student 2 repeats everything and adds another item.
4. Continue around the room until all have added something to the shopping list.

Let's Practice

1. Dictation
1. The instructor will put the food words on the board.
2. The instructor will dictate some measurements, for example: a box of…
3. Students write the measurements.
4. Students complete the sentences with the food words from the board.
5. Students read their sentences to the class.

UNIT 3 – LET'S EAT - LESSON 2 – FOOD PACKAGING AND MEASUREMENTS
STUDENT BOOK PAGE 44

A. Conduct the Let's Practice Activity 2. There's a Carton of Juice in the Refrigerator
1. Prepare in advance several cards with the food vocabulary words printed one per card. Duplicate if necessary to have more than just one card per student.
2. Distribute cards a few to each student.
3. Draw the outline of a refrigerator and freezer and kitchen cabinet on the board.
4. Direct students to place their food cards into the correct place.
5. As students affix their cards to the board with tacky tape, encourage them to make statements, for example: "There is a carton of juice in the refrigerator."
6. Review by having students make statements as the instructor randomly points to the foods.

B. Conduct the Let's Practice Activity 3. Shopping List - Dictation Relay
1. Write a shopping list on a sheet of paper and hang it outside the room on the wall.
2. Divide students into groups of three or pairs. One student from each group/pair will be the Reader while the other student(s) will be the Writer(s).
3. Readers may go out to read the shopping list on the wall.
4. Readers return and dictate the shopping list to their Writer(s).
5. Readers may go out as often as necessary, however, Readers may NOT write down anything, nor take a photo of the list. They must repeat the shopping list from memory.
6. Note which group finishes first.
7. Groups read their finished shopping list to the class while the teacher follows along on the original checking for accuracy.
8. Group with the most accuracy wins.

C. Conduct the Let's Practice Activity 4. Twenty Questions
1. The instructor asks students to think of a food word.   Instructor should leave the room while students confer.
2. When the instructor returns one student says, "We're thinking of a food." [for example, the student is thinking about ice cream]
3. Instructor asks questions which can be answered "yes" or "no" to discover which food the class is thinking about. For example, the instructor may ask:
    a. "Is this food in a package?" [no]   "Is this food cold?" [yes]
    b. "Is this food in the refrigerator?" [no] "Is this food in the freezer?" [yes]
    c. "Is this food ice cream?" [yes]
4. Reverse roles. Instructor thinks of a food and class asks the questions. Do not let students ask only, "Is this food in the cabinet, refrigerator, etc." -or- "Is it ice cream?" "Is it meat?" "Is it oranges?" The idea is to practice formulating questions.

D. Conduct the Let's Practice Activity 5. Scrambled Sentence This is the biblical principle.
Prepare in advance two sets of cards with the words of Matthew 4:4 divided onto

2. There's a Carton of Juice in the Refrigerator
1. The instructor will draw a refrigerator, freezer, and kitchen cabinet on the board.
2. Each student receives some cards with food words.
3. Students place their food cards into the correct place: refrigerator, freezer, or kitchen cabinet.
4. Students make statements about the food, for example: "There is a carton of juice in the refrigerator."

3. Shopping List
1. Students work in groups of three.
2. Each group chooses one student to be the 'reader'.
3. The other 2 students will be 'writers'.
4. The instructor will put a shopping list outside the room on the wall.
5. The readers can go out to read the list, then come back and tell the writers what is on the list. Readers can go in and out as many times as they want. Writers can NOT go out of the room, nor take a photo of the list.
6. Groups read their shopping list to the class.
7. To win, a group must be first finished AND correct. Good Luck!

4. Twenty Questions
1. The instructor asks the class to think about one of the food words.
2. The instructor leaves the room while the class decides which food word to think about.
3. The instructor comes back into the room.
4. The class says, "We're thinking of a food."
5. For example, the class is thinking about ice cream.
6. The instructor asks questions that can be answered with YES or NO to discover which food the class is thinking about.
7. For example, the instructor may ask:
- "Is this food in a package?"   The class says, "No."
- "Is this food cold?"   The class says, "Yes."
- "Is this food for breakfast?"   The class says, "No."
- "Is this food in the refrigerator?   "   "   "No."
- "Is this food in the freezer?"   "   "   "Yes."
- "Is this food ice cream?"   "   "   "Yes!!!"

5. Scrambled Sentence
1. Students make 2 groups.
2. The instructor will give each group a set of cards with the words of a sentence.

UNIT 3 – LET'S EAT - LESSON 2 – FOOD PACKAGING AND MEASUREMENTS
STUDENT BOOK PAGE 45

individual cards as demonstrated by the slash marks:
- Matthew 4:4 - Jesus said, "It is written: / 'Man does not live / on bread alone, / but on every word / that comes from / the mouth of God.'"
- Divide into two groups.
- Students work together to put the sentence into correct order.
- Groups read their sentence to the class.
- The instructor may care to elaborate on the verse.

<u>Review Exercises</u>

<u>2. Shopping List</u>
Answer Key – answers in bold

A **gallon**_____ of ice cream

A **package**_____ of meat

A **can**_____ of soup

A **dozen**_____ eggs

A **carton**_____ of juice

A **box**_____ of crackers

3. Students work in their groups to put the sentence into correct order.
4. Groups read their sentence to the class.

Review Exercises

1. Writing
At home, look at the food in your kitchen cabinet, refrigerator, or freezer. What are your favorite foods? Write a paragraph of 3-4 sentences about your favorite foods.

In my kitchen I have some _____

_____

_____

_____

_____

2. Shopping List
Complete the Shopping List.

1. A _____   of ice cream

2. A _____   of meat

3. A _____   of soup

4. A _____   eggs

5. A _____   of juice

6. A _____   of crackers

3. What's in Your Kitchen?
Look in your kitchen cabinet, refrigerator, and freezer. Write foods that you have in the different packages.

1. A box   ***CRACKERS, COOKIES, PASTA, ZIP LOCK BAGS*** _____

_____

_____

_____

UNIT 3 – LET'S EAT - LESSON 2 – FOOD PACKAGING AND MEASUREMENTS
STUDENT BOOK PAGE 46

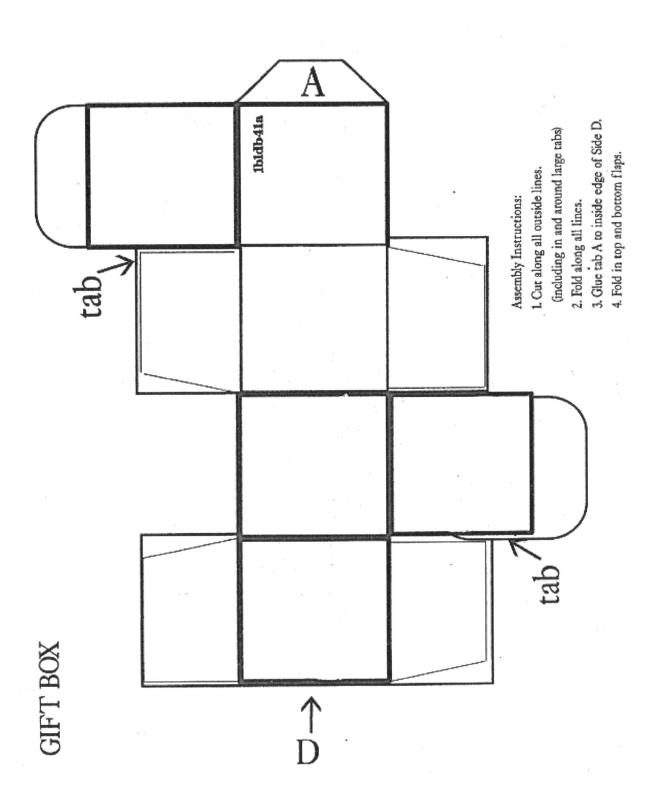

GIFT BOX

Assembly Instructions:
1. Cut along all outside lines.
   (including in and around large tabs)
2. Fold along all lines.
3. Glue tab A to inside edge of Side D.
4. Fold in top and bottom flaps.

2. A can _____

_____

_____

_____

3. A carton _____

_____

_____

_____

4. A package _____

_____

_____

_____

UNIT 4 – SHOPPING - LESSON 1 – CLOTHING SIZE AND FIT
STUDENT BOOK PAGE 47

A. Prayer for Students & Self

B. Lesson Objective and Functions:
- Students will use adjectives to describe the fit of clothing

C. Grammar Structures:
- Using TOO + Adjective

D. Biblical Reference or Principles:
- Genesis 37ff Joseph's Coat of Many Colors

E. Materials & Preparation
1. For Joseph's Coat of Many Colors Biblical Principle Activity, prepare a drawing of a man with a striped coat on a white board or a chart page. Provide 6-8 different colored markers or crayons.
2. For Clothing Boxes Activity, use the box template to prepare sets of FOUR boxes for each small group of students. One box will have sizes, one will be colors, and the third will be articles of clothing, and the fourth will be adjectives describing clothing fit from the vocabulary.
- To prepare the boxes, copy the template onto heavy card stock such as a file folder, and cut out. Alternately, copy the template onto paper, then glue to the file folder for reinforcement and cut out.
- Label the six squares of the boxes with a marker. Use the vocabulary words for colors, sizes, fit adjectives, and articles of clothing. Fold the box along the folding lines, and following the printed instructions, construct the boxes. Tape closed to retain shape.
3. For Vocabulary introduction of colors, use crayons, markers, construction paper, etc.

Introduction
1. Direct students to look at the clothing fit pictures in their books.
2. Ask: "Do you have any clothes that fit like these pictures? What do you do when your clothes fit like this?" [get responses]
3. Say: "Today we are going to learn vocabulary for describing how our clothing fits. We need this vocabulary when we are shopping for clothing in a department store or if we are ordering online."

Introduce New Vocabulary
1. Drill the clothing store vocabulary words with a Repetition Drill 5-6 times each word.
2. Drill the color words with whatever you've brought such as crayons, markers, etc. Identify who is wearing what color in the room.

UNIT 4 - SHOPPING
LESSON 1 – CLOTHING SIZE AND FIT

department store

colors

green   **black**   **blue**   **red**

brown

UNIT 4 – SHOPPING - LESSON 1 – CLOTHING SIZE AND FIT
STUDENT BOOK PAGE 48

A. Introduce Clothing Sizes and Fit
Drill the sizes and fit vocabulary words with a repetition drill 5-6 times each word.

too tight

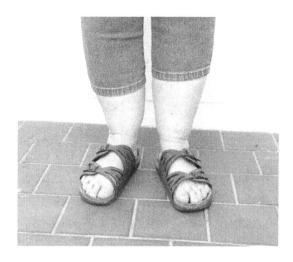

too short

too large

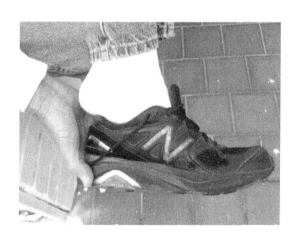

too small

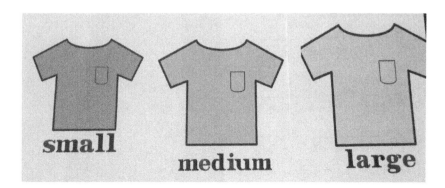

sizes

A. Introduce Articles of Clothing

1. Drill the Articles of Clothing vocabulary words with a repetition drill 5-6 times each word.
2. Ask: "How many pairs of blue jeans do you have?" [get responses]
3. Ask: "What kind of T-shirt do you like? Colored or white? With words and pictures or without?" [get responses]
4. Demonstrate. Instructor draws a picture of his/her favorite T-shirt. Show it to the students and tell why it's your favorite. Have students work with a partner and do the same.

T-shirt

shirt

a pair of blue jeans

a pair of pants

blouse

UNIT 4 – SHOPPING - LESSON 1 – CLOTHING SIZE AND FIT
STUDENT BOOK PAGE 50

Time to Speak

A. Complete *To Do First:*
   1. Introduce the conversation, My Clothes are too Small, under Time to Speak. Have students repeat each line after the instructor. Repeat each line 5-6 times. Strive for a normal, conversational tone rather than an oral reading tone.
   2. Use backward build up for sentences longer than 4 words. Remember to divide sentences into their sound units.
   3. Use correct intonation, stress, and rhythm patterns. Include the following intonation patterns:
   - Statement- the voice starts higher and moves downward like going down a staircase through each sound unit in a statement. When the end of the statement is reached, at the period, the voice falls. The Statement Intonation Pattern is used for Statements which do not require a response.
   - WH-Questions- questions that begin with the WH-Question words: Who, What, Where, When, Why, How, require a response from the listener. The voice begins on a high note, then falls through the middle of the sentence until the last Content word when the voice rises to accent the accented syllable in the last Content word and then falls.

B. Have students complete *To Do Second*.

C. Ask for volunteers to present the Substitutions No. 1-4 for the class.

To Do First: Repeat the conversation after the instructor.

My Clothes are too Small

1.A.   My clothes are **too small**.   Let's go shopping.
   1.B.   O.K.
2.A.   Here's a **medium brown blouse**. I'll try it on.
   2.B.   How does it fit?
3.A.   It fits good.

To Do Second: Speak with a partner. Change the underlined words in the conversation for the Substitutions in No. 1-4 below.

Substitution No. 1

1.A.   too tight
2.A.   small red T-shirt

Substitution No. 2

1.A.   too short
2.A.   large pair of blue jeans

Substitution No. 3

1.A.   too large
2.A.   medium pair of black pants

Substitution No. 4

1.A.   too large
2.A.   small green shirt

UNIT 4 – SHOPPING - LESSON 1 – CLOTHING SIZE AND FIT
STUDENT BOOK PAGE 51

Grammar Foundation

A. Introduce the Grammar Foundation by reading information under Using Too.

B. Complete *To Do First*.

C. Complete *To Do Second*. Go over students' responses.
Answer Key – answers are underlined bold

1. My pants are too tight.
   A. I can wear them.
   B. **I can't wear them.**

2. The blouse is too expensive.
   A. **I can't buy it.**
   B. I can buy it with my credit card.

3. My son is too heavy.
   A. I can pick him up.
   B. **I can't pick him up.**

4. These shoes are too tight.
   A. **I can't wear them.**
   B. I can wear them tomorrow.

5. These jeans are too large.
   A. **I have to return them to the store.**
   B. I can wear them tonight.

Practicing Perfect Pronunciation

Pronounce can and contrast it with can't. Have students repeat each word after the instructor.

Grammar Foundation

Using Too

Too is used in front of Adjectives. It implies a negative result. For example:

The computer is too expensive.	Negative Result – We cannot buy it.
The pants are too big.	Negative Result – The pants don't fit.
The box is too heavy.	Negative Result – I can't pick it up.
The T-shirt is too dirty.	Negative Result – I can't wear it.

To Do First:

Repeat each sentence after the instructor.

To Do Second:

Circle the best result for the sentences.

1. My pants are too tight.   A. I can wear them.
                                                     B. I can't wear them.

2. The blouse is too expensive.   A. I can't buy it.
                                                      B. I can buy it with my credit card.

3. My son is too heavy.   A. I can pick him up.
                                                      B. I can't pick him up.

4. These shoes are too tight.   A. I can't wear them.
                                                      B. I can wear them tomorrow.

5. These jeans are too large.   A. I have to return them to the store.
                                                      B. I can wear them tonight.

~~ Practicing Perfect Pronunciation ~~

Can and Can't - Can is the ability to do something. Can't is the opposite – not able to do something.

UNIT 4 – SHOPPING - LESSON 1 – CLOTHING SIZE AND FIT
STUDENT BOOK PAGE 52

A. Practicing Perfect Pronunciation Continued…
1. After drilling pronunciation of can and can't, ask students to close their eyes.
2. The instructor says either can or can't. Tell students to raise their hand when they hear the word 'can'. Don't raise their hand if the instructor says 'can't'.

B. Practicing 'S' Sounds in Rhythm
1. Draw students' attention to the chant, Suzy's Terrible Togs. Explain that 'togs' is an informal word for clothing.
2. Repeat each line of the chant after the instructor, stretching out the word t-o-o, and the word 'so'.
3. Clap an even rhythm as students perform the chant along with the instructor.

Let's Practice

A. Conduct the Let's Practice Activity 1. Clothing Fit Listening Activity.
1. If possible, record the conversations in advance of the class. If unable, you can simply read the transcript. The answer key below is the transcript. Say the underlined bold words in brackets. For fun, try two different voices for Speakers A and B.
2. Read each conversation 2 times only. Read the underlined word inside each pair of brackets. Students should circle the word in the [brackets] that they hear. Go over student responses.

Answer Key – correct responses are underlined bold.

1.A.   How does the [**blouse** - T-shirt] fit?
1.B.   I think it is too [**small** - short].

Continued next page…

1. Repeat Can and Can't after the instructor.
2. Close your eyes and listen to the instructor. Raise your hand when the instructor says 'Can'. Don't raise your hand if the instructor says 'Can't'.

Practicing 'S' Sounds in Rhythm

Repeat after the instructor.

Suzy's Terrible Togs

by Barbara Kinney Black

Too short, too short, too short,   my jeans are t-o-o short.

Too tight, too tight, too tight,   my blouse is t-o-o tight.

Too small, too small, too small,   my shoes are t-o-o small.

Too large, too large, too large,   my pants are t-o-o large.

My jeans are so short

My blouse is so tight

My shoes are so small

My pants are so large

Too short, too tight, too small, too large.

Too short, too tight, too small, too large.

Too short, too tight, too small, too large.

T-o-o   b-a-d   for Suzy!!

1. Clothing Fit Listening Activity

1. Listen to the conversations.
2. Circle the word in [brackets] that you hear.

1.A.   How does the [blouse - T-shirt] fit?
1.B.   I think it is too [small - short].

UNIT 4 – SHOPPING - LESSON 1 – CLOTHING SIZE AND FIT
STUDENT BOOK PAGE 53

2.A.   How does the [shirt - **T-shirt**] fit?
2.B.   It is too [tight - **short**].
3.A.   How do the [pants - **shoes**] fit?
3.B.   They are too [**tight** – small].
4.A.   How do the [jeans - **pants**] fit?
4.B.   I think they are too [**large** - short].
5.A.   How does the [blouse - **shirt**] fit?
5.B.   It is too [**large** - short].

B. Conduct the Let's Practice Activity 2. Clothing Boxes
    1. Prepare sets of boxes in advance. See instructions under Materials and Preparation.
    2. Divide students into as many small groups as you have 4-box sets for.
    3. Student groups throw down their 4 boxes like dice.
    4. Students make sentences with the words that appear face up on their boxes.
    5. Encourage students to speak the sentences rather than write them. However, one sentence should be written in order to share with the class after the activity.

C. Conduct the Let's Practice Activity 3. Mystery Person
    1. Have each student choose a partner.
    2. The instructor will identify to himself/herself one of the students. Say, "I'm thinking about a student."
    3. The students then must ask questions which the instructor can answer with YES or NO to try and discover which student the instructor is thinking about. For example, a student may ask, "Is this student wearing black pants?" The instructor answers YES or NO.
    4. If a student asks a question such as, "What color pants is the student wearing", the instructor cannot answer this question with just a YES or NO.
    5. After teams have gathered sufficient information through questions, they may guess which student the instructor is thinking about. If they are wrong, that team is out and play continues with remaining teams.
    6. Discourage the constant questions, "Is it Judy?" "Is it Maria?" early in the activity, as this does not practice the language of clothing or constructing questions, but rather turns into a guessing game only.

D. Conduct the Let's Practice activity 4. Play Change the Chair
    1. Direct students to place their chairs in a circle facing in. Remove one chair.
    2. The student without a chair stands in the center of the circle. This student says, "Everyone wearing red, change chairs."
    3. All students wearing red must get up and move to another chair while the student in

2.A.   How does the [shirt - T-shirt] fit?

2.B.   It is too [tight - short].

3.A.   How do the [pants - shoes] fit?

3.B.   They are too [tight – small].

4.A.   How do the [jeans - pants] fit?

4.B.   I think they are too [large - short].

5.A.   How does the [blouse - shirt] fit?

5.B.   It is too [large - short].

2. Clothing Boxes

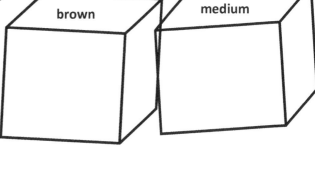

1. Work in a small group.
2. The instructor will give you 4 boxes. Throw down the boxes on the table.
3. Make a sentence with the words on the top of the boxes. For example: 'The medium, brown blouse is too small.'
4. Share one of your sentences with the class.

3. Mystery Person

1. Work with a partner.
2. The instructor will think of one student.
3. Ask questions to the instructor to learn which student the instructor is thinking about. The instructor can only answer your question with YES or NO. For example, "Is this student wearing black pants?" Instructor will answer YES or NO.
4. When you think you know which student the instructor is thinking about, tell the instructor you want to guess.

4. Play Change the Chair

1. Make a large circle of chairs with one less chair than students.
2. The student without a chair stands in the center.
3. The student in the center says, "Everyone wearing red, change chairs."
4. Everyone wearing red clothing must get up and move to another chair. The student in the center takes a chair.
5. The student without a chair stands in the center and gives the next direction.

UNIT 4 – SHOPPING - LESSON 1 – CLOTHING SIZE AND FIT
STUDENT BOOK PAGE 54

the center takes one of the empty chairs.

4. The student left without a chair stands in the center and gives the next direction.

5. Enforce a 'no running or pushing' policy.

E. Conduct the Let's Practice Activity 5. Joseph's Coat. This is the Biblical Principle.

1. Prepare in advance. Draw on the white board or a piece of chart paper a man with a striped coat. See example.

2. Distribute different colored markers or crayons to every student.

3. Introduce the activity. Take a colored marker, for example, red, and color one of the stripes. Say: "Joseph had a coat of many colors. His coat was red."

4. Direct Student 1 to come and color another strip, for example, blue. Student 1 repeats, "Joseph had a coat of many colors. His coat was red and blue."

5. Continue until all have colored a stripe.

6. Consider sharing the story of Joseph and his coat of many colors.

B. Check the Review Exercises in the next class for 2. Scrambled Sentences. Any grammatically correct sentence which uses all the words is acceptable.

Answer Key

1. My son is wearing a red T-shirt and a pair of blue jeans.

2. My black pants are too tight.

3. My green pants are too large and too short.

4.   I am wearing a black T-shirt and a pair of white pants.

5. Joseph's Coat – Add On Game

1. The instructor will draw a man with a striped coat on the board.
2. Student 1 comes to the board and colors one stripe with a red marker. Student 1 says, "Joseph had a coat of many colors. His coat was red."
3. Student 2 comes and colors another stripe blue. Student 2 repeats, "Joseph had a coat of many colors. His coat was red and blue." Repeat until all stripes are colored.

Review Exercises

1. Write Sentences

Write 5 sentences about the clothing your family is wearing, for example: My daughter is wearing a white shirt and a pair of blue jeans. Share your sentences in class.

1. ***My daughter is wearing a white shirt and a pair of blue jeans.***

2. _____

3. _____

4. _____

5. _____

2. Scrambled Sentences

Unscramble the sentences and put them into correct order. Use all the words.

1. my   is   a   and   pair   jeans   T-shirt   wearing
   of   a   blue   red   son   ***My son is wearing***

_____

2. pants   tight   black   too   my   are

_____

3. pants   my   too   are   and   green   too   large
   short

_____

4. pants   wearing   a   I   and   am   a   of   white
   black   pair   T-shirt

_____

_____

UNIT 5 – HOUSING - LESSON 1 – CHOOSING HOUSING
STUDENT BOOK PAGE 55

A. Prayer for Students & Self

B. Lesson Objective and Functions:
• Describing types of housing and housing features

C. Grammar Structures:
• Articles A and AN

D. Biblical Reference or Principles:
• Matthew 8:20: Jesus replied, "Foxes have holes and birds of the air have nests, but the son of Man has no place to lay his head."

E. Materials & Preparation:
• Real estate section of a newspaper

Introduction
1. Pantomime reading the real estate classified section of newspaper for houses to rent. Read ads aloud and comment on the prices.
2. Ask students: "Who lives in a house? Who lives in an apartment? Who lives in a mobile home? Do you rent your house or did you buy your house?"
3. Say: " Today we are going to talk about moving."

Introduce New Vocabulary
1. Have students open to Unit 5 – Housing; Lesson 1 – Choosing Housing.
2. Introduce the 4 different types of housing with a repetition drill.
3. For each type of housing, ask: "Who would like to live in this type of housing? Why? "In what neighborhood can you find this type of housing?"

UNIT 5 - HOUSING
LESSON 1 – CHOOSING HOUSING

TYPES OF HOUSING

apartment

townhouse

house

mobile home

UNIT 5 – HOUSING - LESSON 1 – CHOOSING HOUSING
STUDENT BOOK PAGE 56

1. Introduce moving words with a repetition drill.
2. Ask questions related to the pictures, for example:
- "When was the last time you moved?"
- "Did you move yourself or hire a company to move you?"
- "How did you find out about the place you are now living?"
- "Do you rent or do you own your house?"
- "How many bedrooms and bathrooms do you have?"

to move

for rent sign

above – bedroom

above right – bathroom

right – lease

To Do   May 1

Lease is up

Move

UNIT 5 – HOUSING - LESSON 1 – CHOOSING HOUSING
STUDENT BOOK PAGE 57

Time to Speak

A. Complete *To Do First:*
   1. Introduce the conversation, It's Time to Move, under Time to Speak. Have students repeat each line after the instructor. Repeat each line 5-6 times. Strive for a normal, conversational tone rather than an oral reading tone.
   2. Use backward build up for sentences longer than 4 words. Remember to divide sentences into their sound units.
   3. Use correct intonation, stress, and rhythm patterns. Include the following intonation patterns:
   - Statement- the voice starts higher and moves downward like going down a staircase through each sound unit in a statement. When the end of the statement is reached, at the period, the voice falls. The Statement Intonation Pattern is used for Statements which do not require a response.
   - WH-Questions- questions that begin with the WH-Question words: Who, What, Where, When, Why, How, require a response from the listener. The voice begins on a high note, then falls through the middle of the sentence until the last Content word when the voice rises to accent the accented syllable in the last Content word and then falls.

B. Have students complete *To Do Second*.

C. Ask for volunteers to present the Substitutions No. 1-3 for the class.

To Do First: Repeat the conversation after the instructor.

It's Time to Move

1.A.   My lease is up. I have to move.
   1.B.   Oh, there's **an apartment** for rent next to me.
2.A.   How many bedrooms does it have?
   2.B.   It has **two** bedrooms.
3.A.   That's good. How much is the rent?
   3.B.   It's **$950** a month.
4.A.   O.K. Let's go see it.

To Do Second: Speak with a partner. Change the <u>underlined words</u> in the conversation for the Substitutions in No. 1-3 below.

Substitution No. 1
   1.B.   a house
   2.B.   three
   3.B. $1,200

Substitution No. 2

   1.B.   a mobile home
   2.B.   two
   3.B. $800

Substitution No. 3

   1.B.   a townhouse
   2.B.   three
   3.B. $1,150

UNIT 5 – HOUSING - LESSON 1 – CHOOSING HOUSING
STUDENT BOOK PAGE 58

Grammar Foundation

A. Introduce the Grammar Foundation by reading information under Using A Vs. AN.

B. Complete *To Do First* by having students repeat each example phrase, including: an apartment, an understanding, a useless car, etc.

C. Complete *To Do Second* by doing exercises 1-3. together as a class. Have student pairs complete exercises 4-8.

D. Complete *To Do* Third by going over responses asking which grammar rule applies, for example, for No. 1, use rule 3: Use the article AN before all Singular Nouns beginning with the vowel letters.

Answer Key – in bold
1. I have __*an*__ orange rug.
2. I live in ____**a**__ mobile home on the corner of Sheridan Street and Palm Avenue.
3. That townhouse is painted **an**____ ugly color.
4. There is ____**an** apartment building on the corner of University Drive and Pines Boulevard.
5. I live in __**a**____ two bedroom apartment.
6. There is ____**a**__ university on the corner of Palm Avenue and Johnson Street.
7. ____**An**_ uncle of mine lives next door.
8. There is ____**an** ice cream cone in the dish on the dining table.

Practicing Perfect Pronunciation

Introduce the Statement Intonation Pattern by reading the information. Demonstrate.

Grammar Foundation

Using A Vs. An

1. 'A' and 'AN' are called Articles. They are used in front of Singular Nouns.
2. Use the article "A" before All Singular Nouns beginning with a consonant letter. For example: a house; a car; a mobile home; a newspaper; a townhouse.
3. Use the article "AN" before all Singular Nouns beginning with the vowel letters: "A, E, I, or O." For example:

     an apartment   an example   an ice cream cone   an oven

4. For Singular Nouns beginning with the vowel letter "U", use the article "AN" if the "U" sound is like the sound at the beginning of the words "uncle" or "ugly." For example:

     an understanding   an ugly house   an umbrella

5. Use the article "A" if the "U" sound is like the sound at the beginning of the words "university" or "usual". For example:

     a useless car   a unique experience

To Do First: Repeat the example words after the instructor.

To Do Second: Complete the sentences using the correct Article A or AN.

1. I have ___***an***___ orange rug.
2. I live in _____ mobile home on the corner of Sheridan Street and Palm Avenue.
3. That townhouse is painted _____ ugly color.
4. There is _____ apartment building on the corner of University Drive and Pines Boulevard.
5. I live in _____ two bedroom apartment.
6. There is _____ university on the corner of Palm Avenue and Johnson Street.
7. _____ uncle of mine lives next door.
8. There is _____ ice cream cone in the dish on the dining table.

To Do Third: Share your responses with the class.

~~ *Practicing Perfect Pronunciation* ~~

The Statement Intonation Pattern is used for Statements – sentences that end with a period. The voice goes down on each sound unit and down at the end of the statement.

UNIT 5 – HOUSING - LESSON 1 – CHOOSING HOUSING
STUDENT BOOK PAGE 59

A. Demonstrate the Statement Intonation Pattern by repeating the statements from the conversation. Remember to divide the statements into their sound units. For each sound unit, the voice starts higher and moves steadily down to the comma, then starts higher again and moves steadily down to the period. Have students repeat each line 2-3 times.

B. Demonstrate how to draw an arrow following the sentence below to indicate where the voice is high, and then taper down through the sentence where the voice goes down.

"A two bedroom apartment, $950 a month."

Let's Practice

A. Complete the Let's Practice Activity 1. Dictation
1. Demonstrate on board how to write the dollar amounts.
2. Dictate the dollar amounts from the conversation, for example: "nine hundred fifty dollars". Include:
3. $950; $1,200; $800, $1,150. Add 2 more of your choice. _____
4. Students respond by writing in numeral form, for example: $150.00.
5. Go over student responses by having volunteers write the amounts on the board for each response.

B. Complete the Let's Practice Activity 2. Real Estate Ads Cloze. Read the ads below as many times as students request. In order to simulate a more 'real life' listening activity, speak at a normal speed. Do all four ads before repeating.

Answer Key – in bold

Ad Number 1: Two **bedroom** apartment for rent, $1,325 a **month**. Call 954.**435.1225**.

Ad Number 2: Three bedroom house for **rent, $1,450** a month. Call 954.432.9877.

Continued next page...

The easiest way to hear the sound units is by listening to your instructor. So, repeat each phrase after the instructor. Listen for the voice going down.

1. A two bedroom apartment, $950 a month.

2. A two bedroom mobile home, $800 a month.

3. A two bedroom mobile home, $750 a month.

4. A three bedroom house, $1,300 a month.

5. A three bedroom townhouse, $1,175 a month.

Listen again to the instructor read the sentences. Draw a line to show where the voice goes down. The instructor will demonstrate.

Let's Practice

1. Dictation
The instructor will dictate some dollar amounts. Write the amount you hear below. For example, if you hear, "One hundred fifty dollars," you will write: $150.00.

1._____   4._____

2._____   5._____

3._____   6._____

2. Real Estate Ads Cloze Activity
Listen to the instructor read the ads. Write the missing words you hear on the lines.

Ad No. 1: Two ___**bedroom**___ apartment for rent, $1,325 a _ _____. Call 954-_____.

Ad No. 2: Three bedroom house for _____, $_____ ___ a month. Call 954-432-9877.

UNIT 5 – HOUSING - LESSON 1 – CHOOSING HOUSING
STUDENT BOOK PAGE 60

Ad Number 3: **One** bedroom mobile home for rent, $700 a month. Call **954.432.7781**.

Ad Number 4: Four bedroom **house** for rent, three bathrooms, $1,800 a **month**. Call **954.435.3351**.

C. Complete the Let's Practice Activity 3. Choose Housing for Marie and Jean – Group Activity

1. Have students work in groups of 3 or in pairs.
2. Have students turn to the activity in their books.
3. Read over the 6 housing choices as a class.
4. Each group selects which apartment would be best for Marie and Jean.
5. Note that this activity helps to develop students' critical thinking skills.
6. Go over student responses. Explain there is no single correct answer.
7. Ask students why they chose the responses they did.
8. Instructor demonstrates his/her own critical thinking process by choosing an option for Marie and Jean then explaining their reasons for choosing that particular option. By explaining the instructor's reasoning process, students are introduced to the instructor's cultural background and values.

Ad No. 3: _____ bedroom mobile home for rent, $700 a month.
Call _____ .

Ad No. 4: Four bedroom _____ for rent, three bathrooms, $1,800 a
_____ . Call _____ .

3. Choose Housing for Marie and Jean – Group Activity

Marie and Jean's lease is up. They have to move. Here's a list of some places they can choose.

1. Work with a group of 3 students.
2. Choose the best new home for Marie and Jean.
3. Tell the class which home you chose and what reasons you chose that home.

Housing	Rent	Neighborhood	Features
1. apartment	$900	Cooper City	2 bedrooms
2. mobile home	$950	Pembroke Pines	1 bedroom
3. house	$975	Weston	3 bedrooms
4. townhouse	$925	Hollywood	1 bedroom
5. house	$1,125	Pembroke Pines	4 bedrooms
6. mobile home	$800	Miramar	2 bedrooms

Which housing would you choose for Jean and Marie? _____

_____

Why? _____

UNIT 5 – HOUSING - LESSON 1 – CHOOSING HOUSING
STUDENT BOOK PAGE 61

D. Complete the Let's Practice Activity 4. Our Favorite House – Group Discussion
1. Demonstrate: The instructor describes his/her house to the group. Alternately, use the following example: "I live in a house. It has 3 bedrooms, 2 bathrooms, and a garage for 2 cars. It has a large yard with trees. I like my house because it is large and it costs only $650 a month."
2. Students work in a small group or in pairs.
3. Each student has 2 minutes to describe their house to the group.
4. Optional Extension: Have pairs join with other pairs to make a small group of 4. Original partners share their partner's house description with the group. Continue until all have participated.

E. Play the Let's Practice Activity 5. Play Beat the Cat
  Note this is the biblical principle.
1. Prepare in advance. For complete instructions, see the Activity Bank.
2. Use this puzzle sentence, a paraphrase of the verse Matthew 8:20: "Foxes have holes and birds have nests, but Jesus has no house."
3. After completion of the puzzle, the instructor puts Matthew 8:20 on the board and students repeat after the instructor 3 times.
4. Matthew 8:20: Jesus replied, "Foxes have holes and birds of the air have nests, but the son of Man has no place to lay his head."
5. The instructor may choose to comment on the meaning of the verse.
6.

Review Exercises

Answer Key – in bold
Number 1
Two bedroom apartment for rent, in Cooper City, $1,300 a month. Call 954.435.1355.

Number 2
Three bedroom house for rent, in Pembroke Pines, $1,550 a month, Call 954.431.5220.

4. Our Favorite House – Group Discussion

1. Work with a small group.

2. In 2 minutes, describe your house to the group. For example: I live in a house. It has 3 bedrooms, 2 bathrooms, and a garage for 2 cars. It has a large yard with trees. I like my house because it is large and it costs only $650 a month.

5. Play Beat the Cat

1. This game is like the TV show Wheel of Fortune. The instructor will put a puzzle on the board.

2. Students take turns guessing consonants.

3. If the consonant is in the puzzle, the instructor will write it on the line. If the consonant is NOT in the puzzle, the instructor will draw part of a cat.

4. Continue until only vowels are left in the puzzle.

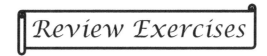

Review Exercises

1. Read Housing Ads

Read each real estate ad. Answer the questions about the ads.

Number 1

Two bedroom apartment
for rent, in Cooper
City, $1,300 a month.
Call 954.435.1355.

Number 2

Three bedroom house
for rent, in Pembroke
Pines, $1,550 a month,
Call 954.431.5220.

UNIT 5 – HOUSING - LESSON 1 – CHOOSING HOUSING
STUDENT BOOK PAGE 62

Number 3

Two bedroom mobile home for rent, in Hollywood, $775 a month, parking for 3 cars.
Call 954.983.8700.

1. How much is the rent for the mobile home? __**$775**__
2. Which ad has parking for 3 cars? __**3**__
3. Where is the apartment? __**Cooper City**__
4. How many bedrooms does the house have? __**3**__
5. How much is the rent for the house? __**$1,550**__
6. Which ad has the highest rent? __**2**__
7. Which ad has the lowest rent? __**3**__
8. Where is the house? __**Pembroke Pines**__

Number 3

Two bedroom mobile
home for rent, in
Hollywood, $775 a
month, parking for 3
cars. Call 954.983.8700.

1. How much is the rent for the mobile home?_____

2. Which ad has parking for 3 cars?   _____

3. Where is the apartment?   _____

4. How many bedrooms does the house have?   _____

5. How much is the rent for the house?_____

6. Which ad has the highest rent?   _____

7. Which ad has the lowest rent?   _____

8. Where is the house?   _____

UNIT 5 – HOUSING - LESSON 2 – MOVING
STUDENT BOOK PAGE 63

A. Prayer for Students & Self

B. Lesson Objective and Functions:
• Students will describe positioning of home furnishings

C. Grammar Structures:
• Demonstratives: This, That, These, Those
• Questions with Where + Do

D. Biblical Reference or Principles:
• Hebrews 3:4: Many people can build houses, but only God made everything.

E. Materials & Preparation:
1. For Grammar Foundation Activity Using Demonstratives – create 8 ½ x 11 signs with one furniture word on each sign.
2. For Furniture Bingo Listening Activity – create Bingo cards and provide Smarties candy rolls for Bingo chips. See Activity Bank for instruction and Bingo card template.
3. For Mover/Home Owner Role Play – create 8 ½ x 11 signs one for each of the rooms of the house from the vocabulary. Place around the classroom designating rooms of a house.
4. For Scrambled Sentence Activity: Write the phrases of Hebrews: 3:4 as divided by slash marks onto individual 3x5 index cards. Create two sets of cards for two groups of students.

Introduction
1. Show the picture Moving Men on the last page of the the teacher guide for this unit. Ask: "What are they doing?" [get student responses].
2. Say: "When it's time to move, do you hire a moving company or move yourself with help from family and friends." [get student responses].
3. Draw a picture on board of a room in your house. Write the name of the room. Draw and label small squares for each piece of furniture in that room. Describe the room to the students. For example: "This is my living room. There is a sofa and a TV. There is a coffee table and two chairs. There are 3 windows. There are curtains on the windows."
4. 2. Say: "Tonight we are going to learn language for moving into a new house and putting furniture into the rooms."

Introduce New Vocabulary
1. Have students open to Unit 5 – Housing; Lesson 2 – Moving In.
2. Introduce the rooms of the floor plan with a repetition drill.
3. For each room ask: "Which room do you spend the most time in? What do you do in there?

UNIT 5 - HOUSING
LESSON 2 – MOVING IN

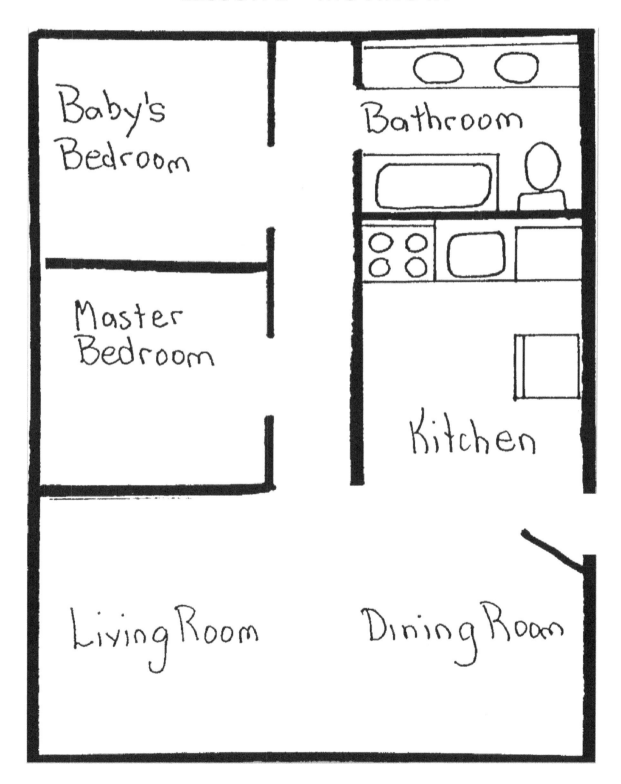

UNIT 5 – HOUSING - LESSON 2 – MOVING
STUDENT BOOK PAGE 64

1. Introduce each moving word with a repetition drill.
2. Ask students questions about each item, for example:
- Describe your dining table.
- Do you like to read?
- How many chairs do you have?
- What's your favorite color for towels?
3. After each word is introduced, write on the board.
4. Practice the difference between pronunciation of /s/ and /z/ on the word endings:

/s/ ending sounds	/z/ ending sounds
Books	beds, sofas, chairs, tables, towels

5. Help students produce the /z/ sound by telling them to make the sound of a buzzing bee.

baby's room

living room

kitchen

master bedroom

bathroom

dining room

UNIT 5 – HOUSING - LESSON 2 – MOVING
STUDENT BOOK PAGE 65

1. Continue introducing rooms vocabulary with a repetition drill.
2. Ask students to name other rooms in their houses.

sofa

crib

chair

books

towels

table

UNIT 5 – HOUSING - LESSON 2 – MOVING
STUDENT BOOK PAGE 66

Time to Speak

A. Complete *To Do First:*

1. Introduce the conversation, Moving In, under Time to Speak. Have students repeat each line after the instructor. Repeat each line 5-6 times. Strive for a normal, conversation tone rather than an oral reading tone.

2. Use backward build up for sentences longer than 4 words. Remember to divide sentences into their sound units.

3. Use correct intonation, stress, and rhythm patterns. Include the following intonation patterns:

- Statement (the voice starts higher and moves downward like going down a staircase through each sound unit in a statement. When the end of the statement is reached, at the period, the voice falls).

- WH-Questions (the voice begins on a high note with the WH-Question word, then falls through the middle of the sentence until the last content word when the voice rises to accent the accented syllable in the last content word and then falls).

B. Have students complete *To Do Second.* Call on individual students to read the conversation after each substitution has been drilled.

Grammar Foundation

A. Introduce the Grammar Foundation by completing *To Do First.* Read the information about the Demonstratives (next page).

Time to Speak

To Do First: Repeat the conversation after the instructor.
<u>Moving In</u>

Speaker A: the moving company employee
Speaker B: the home owner

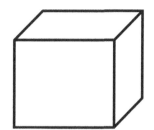

1.A.　　Where do you want **this bed**?
　　1.B.　　**That bed** goes in the **master bedroom**.
2.A.　　Where do you want **these chairs**?
　　2.B.　　**Those chairs** go in the **dining room**.

To Do Second: Speak with a partner. Change the <u>underlined words</u> in the conversation for the Substitutions No. 1-2 below.

<u>Substitution No. 1</u>
1.A.　　Where do you want **this sofa**?
　　1.B.　　**That sofa** goes in the **living room**.
2.A.　　Where do you want **these books**?
　　2.B.　　**Those books** go in the **baby's room**.

Moving In

<u>Substitution No. 2</u>
1.A.　　Where do you want **this table**?
　　1.B.　　**That table** goes in the **kitchen**.
2.A.　　Where do you want **these towels**?
　　2.B.　　**Those towels** go in the **bathroom.**

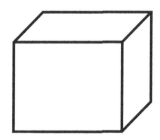

To Do Third: Partners present their conversations to the class.

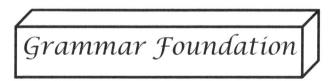

Grammar Foundation

To Do First: Read the information about Demonstratives. Repeat each demonstrative after the instructor.

UNIT 5 – HOUSING - LESSON 2 – MOVING
STUDENT BOOK PAGE 67

B. Conduct the Grammar Foundation Activity Using Demonstratives, _To Do Second_.
1. Prepare in advance: 8 ½ x 11 signs, one each, write in large letters, the furniture vocabulary words. Place the signs around the classroom where all can see.
2. Demonstrate the Activity. The instructor stands next to one word, for example, 'chair.' The instructor says, "THIS chair."
3. The instructor moves away from the chair, points back to it and says, "THAT chair."
4. Repeat with all vocabulary words using the correct Demonstratives: This, That, These, or Those. Have students repeat along with the instructor.

C. Have students complete _To Do Third._ Instructor demonstrate.

D. Have students complete _To Do Fourth_ by reading the information about Where + Do (on the next page).

Using DEMONSTRATIVES - THIS, THAT, THESE, THOSE

DEMONSTRATIVES are used with nouns to explain which noun we are speaking about. THIS and THAT are used with Singular Nouns while THESE and THOSE are used with Plural Nouns.

- THIS is used when the noun is in the speaker's possession or near to the speaker.
- THAT is used when the noun is not in the speaker's possession or not near to the speaker.
- THESE is used when the plural nouns are in the speaker's possession or near to the speaker.
- THOSE is used when the plural nouns are not in the speaker's possession or near to the speaker.

To Do Second:
1. The instructor will place the vocabulary words around the room.
2. The instructor will stand next to a word, for example, 'chair'. The instructor will say, "this chair."
3. The instructor will move across the room and point to the chair. The instructor will say, "that chair."
4. The instructor will repeat with all the Vocabulary words using This, That, These, or Those. Students repeat along with the instructor.

To Do Third:
1. Practice with a partner. Use your books and your pencils.
2. Student 1 picks up one book and says, "this book." Student 1 puts the book down on the other side of the table, points to the book and says, "that book."
3. Student 2 picks up two pencils and says, "these pencils." Student 2 puts the pencils down on the other side of the table, points to the pencils and says, "those pencils."
4. Continue until both partners have practiced all Demonstratives.

To Do Fourth:
1. Read the information about Where + Do.
2. Repeat the example sentences after the instructor.

UNIT 5 – HOUSING - LESSON 2 – MOVING
STUDENT BOOK PAGE 68

Have students repeat the example sentences under Where + Do after the instructor. Repeat each at least 2 times.

Let's Practice

A. Conduct the Let's Practice Activity 1. Dictation
   1. Have students open their books to the activity.
   2. Have students repeat each of the room names after the instructor.
   3. The instructor will say the name of a furniture word, for example, "bed". Students write the word 'bed' under the Bedroom column.
   4. Repeat with each of the furniture words.
   5. Go over student responses by having students make statements, for example: "I put the bed in the bedroom."

B. Conduct the Let's Practice Activity 2. Furniture Bingo
   1. Prepare in advance. Create different Furniture Bingo cards using the template in the Activity Bank.   Write furniture words in the grid spaces.
   2. Get something to use for Bingo chips, for example, a bag of Smarties candy rolls. Alternately, students can use coins or tear up small pieces of paper. Discourage writing on the Bingo card.
   3. To play bingo, point to a picture of one of the furniture words, for example, a table.
   4. Students look for the word 'table' on their Bingo cards and place a Bingo chip.
   5. When students get 3 Bingo chips in a row horizontally, vertically, or diagonally, they should shout "Bingo!"
   6. The instructor will ask which words they have to check accuracy.
   7. Keep score on board. Clear their boards after every win.

Questions with WHERE + DO

WHERE + DO is used to ask about the location for something.

Where + Do/Does + Subject + Main Verb + Object

Where	do	you	want	this bed?
Where	do	you	want	these chairs?
Where	do	you and Tom	want	these desks?
Where	do	the students	want	these books?
Where	does	John	want	these towels?
Where	does	Marie	want	these dishes?
Where	does	your wife	want	this sofa?

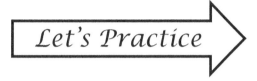

Let's Practice

1. Dictation

The instructor will say the name of a furniture word, for example, 'bed'. Write the word under the correct room. Write 'bed' under the Bedroom.

Bedroom	Living Room	Kitchen	Bathroom
Bed			

2. Furniture Bingo

1. The instructor will give you a Furniture Bingo card and some candy. Use the candy for 'Bingo chips.'
2. The instructor will point to a picture of some furniture, for example, a table.
3. Students look for the word 'table' on their Bingo cards and place a Bingo chip.
4. When students get 3 Bingo chips in a row, shout "Bingo". The instructor will ask you what words you have.

UNIT 5 – HOUSING - LESSON 2 – MOVING
STUDENT BOOK PAGE 69

C. Conduct the Let's Practice Activity 3. Rearrange the Furniture – Listening Activity
1. Have students tear a piece of paper into 8 small pieces. Write the following furniture words one on each paper: crib, bed, chair, table, sofa, TV, books, and towels.
2. Have students turn to the floor plan in their book.
3. The instructor gives a command, for example: 'Put the sofa in the living room." Students will place their 'sofa' paper into the living room.

D. Conduct the Let's Practice Activity 4. Mover/Home Owner – Role Play
1. Prepare in advance. Make 8 ½ x 11" signs one for each of the rooms introduced in the vocabulary. Place these signs around the classroom to delineate rooms.
2. Pair students. Have them use the same small furniture papers they created for the previous activity Rearrange the Furniture.
3. Student 1 is the Mover and Student 2 is the Home Owner.
4. The Mover asks the Home Owner, for example: "Where do you want this table?" The Home Owner replies, "Put that table in the dining room." The Mover takes the table paper and puts it into the dining room.
5. Continue until all furniture has been placed in the room.
6. Change roles and repeat.

E. Conduct the Let's Practice Activity 5. Scrambled Sentence
Note this is the Biblical Principle. Have students put the scrambled verse into correct order. Use the verse Hebrews 3:4. Students read their completed verse to the class.

can build / made everything / many people / houses, but only God

Many people   can build   houses, but only God   made everything.

3. Rearrange the Furniture – Listening Activity

1. Tear a piece of paper into 7 small pieces.
2. Write the following furniture words one on each paper: crib, bed, chair, table, sofa, TV, books.
3. Open your book to the apartment floor plan.
4. The instructor will give a command, for example: "put the sofa in the living room." Students will place their 'sofa' paper into the living room.

4. Mover/Home Owner - Role Play

1. The instructor will place room signs around the classroom. Work with a partner. Use the small furnitue papers from Rearrange the Furniture activity.
2. Student 1 is the Mover. Student 2 is the Home Owner.
3. The Mover asks the Home Owner, for example: "Where do you want this table?"
4. The Home Owner says, "Put that table in the dining room."
5. The Mover takes the table paper and puts it into the dining room.
6. Continue until all furniture has been placed in the room.
7. Change roles and repeat.

5. Scrambled Sentence

1. Below you will see the words for a sentence.
2. Put the words into correct order.   Write it on the line.
3. Read the sentence. It is from Hebrews 3:4 in the Bible.

can build / made everything   / many people / houses, but only God

_____

_____

UNIT 5 – HOUSING - LESSON 2 – MOVING
STUDENT BOOK PAGE 70

Review Exercises

Assign Review Exercises for homework. Go over the instructions to ensure students understand how to complete the activity.

Using This, That, These, and Those

Complete the dialogue. Use this, that, these, or those.

Teacher Key - answers in bold

1.A. Where do you want **_this_** bed?
   1.B. Put **that** bed in the master bedroom.
2.A. Where do you want **these** chairs?
   2.B. Put **those** chairs in the dining room.
3.A. Where do you want **this** TV?
   3.B. Put **that** TV in the living room.
4.A. Where do you want **these** curtains?
   4.B. Put **those** curtains in the kitchen.
5.A. Where do you want **these** towels?
   5.B. Put **those** towels in the bathroom.
6.A. Where do you want **these** books?
   6.B. Put **those** books in the living room.
7.A. Where do you want **this** crib?
   7.B. Put **that** crib in the baby's bedroom.
8.A. Where do you want **these** pictures?
   8.B. Put **those** pictures in the dining room.
9.A. Where do you want **this** TV?
   9.B. Put **that** TV in the master bedroom.
10.A. Where do you want **this** sofa?
   10.B. Put **that** sofa in the living room.

Review Exercises

Using This, That, These, and Those

Complete the conversation. Use this, that, these, or those.

1.A. Where do you want **_this_** bed?

   1.B. Put _____bed in the master bedroom.

2.A. Where do you want _____chairs?

   2.B. Put _____chairs in the dining room.

3.A. Where do you want _____TV?

   3.B. Put_____TV in the living room.

4.A. Where do you want _____curtains?

   4.B. Put   _____curtains in the kitchen.

5.A. Where do you want _____towels?

   5.B. Put   _____towels in the bathroom.

6.A. Where do you want _____books?

   6.B. Put   _____books in the living room.

7.A. Where do you want _____crib?

   7.B. Put _____crib in the baby's bedroom.

8.A. Where do you want _____pictures?

   8.B. Put _____pictures in the dining room.

9.A. Where do you want _____TV?

   9.B. Put _____TV in the master bedroom.

10.A. Where do you want _____sofa?

   10.B. Put _____sofa in the living room.

UNIT 5 – HOUSING – LESSON 2 – MOVING
STUDENT BOOK PAGE 71

2. Write Sentences about your Furniture

Write sentences about your furniture in your house. Use this, that, these, and those.
For example:

1. ***I put that bed in my bedroom***. _____

2. _____

3. _____

4. _____

5. _____

3. Draw a Floor Plan of your House

1. Draw a floor plan of the house or apartment where you live. Use the example floor plan in the book.   Share your floor plan with the class.

UNIT 5 – HOUSING - LESSON 3 – CLEANING HOUSE
STUDENT BOOK PAGE 72

A. Prayer for Students & Self

B. Lesson Objective and Functions:
• Describing location of cleaning products in the home

C. Grammar Structures:
• Imperative Commands for cleaning house: wash, do, sweep, take out
• Prepositions of Location

D. Biblical Reference or Principles:
• Luke 15:8-10: "Suppose a woman who has ten silver coins loses one of them. What does she do? She lights a lamp, sweeps her house, and looks carefully everywhere until she finds it. When she finds it, she calls her friends and neighbors together. 'Rejoice with me,' she tells them, 'for I have found the coin I lost!' In the same way, I tell you, the angels of God rejoice over one sinner who repents."

E. Materials & Preparation:
• For Verbs in the Bag Activity prepare 3x5 index cards with the cleaning commands one on each card, for example: sweep the floor. Use commands from the conversation. Provide a brown paper bag or other container nontransparent to hold the Verb Cards.
• For Cleaning Tasks and Products Mix & Match Activity prepare 3x5 index cards with cleaning commands, for example: 'sweep the floor' and the cleaning products or tools to match, for example: 'broom.'
• For The Lost Coin Pantomime prepare 10 $1,000 bills on 3x5 index cards. Bring a broom, cell phone, and a lamp to class. Alternately, dim the lights in the room or use a flash light.

Introduction
1. The instructor pantomimes cleaning house. Talk to yourself about how much cleaning you have to do today, how little time you have, and how dirty the house is.
2. Ask: "Who likes to clean the house?" [get student response]
• "What cleaning jobs do you like to do?" [get student response]
• "What cleaning jobs do you NOT like to do?" [get student response]
3. Say: "Tonight we are going to learn vocabulary for talking about cleaning the house."

Introduce New Vocabulary
1. Have students open to Unit 5 – Housing; Lesson 3 – Cleaning House.
2. Introduce the 4 cleaning tasks using a repetition drill.
3. For each task, ask: Who does the task in students' homes?
4. "How do you divide the cleaning tasks in your home?"

Unit 5 - Housing
LESSON 3 – CLEANING HOUSE

sweep the floor

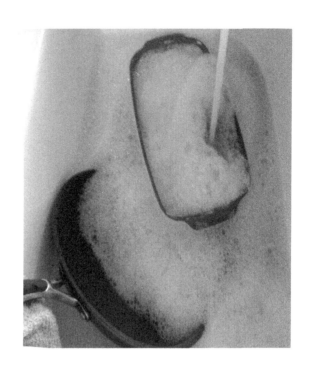

do the dishes

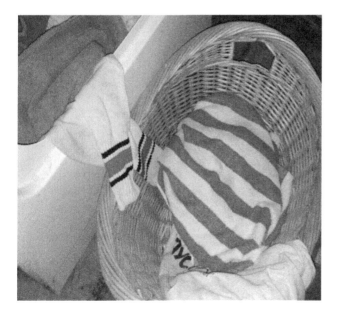

do the laundry

take out the trash

UNIT 5 – HOUSING - LESSON 3 – CLEANING HOUSE
STUDENT BOOK PAGE 73

1. Introduce each cleaning product using a repetition drill. Have students repeat at least 5-6 times after the instructor.
2. Continue with the 3 storage locations: under the sink, in the cabinet, and in the closet.

laundry detergent

dish detergent – under the sink

broom

trash bags

in the closet

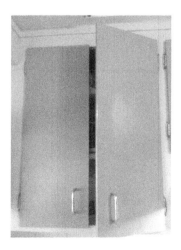

in the cabinet

UNIT 5 – HOUSING - LESSON 3 – CLEANING HOUSE
STUDENT BOOK PAGE 74

Time to Speak

A. Complete *To Do First:*
   1. Introduce the conversation under Time to Speak.   Have students repeat each line after the instructor. Repeat each line 5-6 times. Strive for a normal, conversation tone rather than an oral reading tone.
   2. Use backward build up for sentences longer than 4 words. Remember to divide sentences into their sound units.
   3. Use correct intonation, stress, and rhythm patterns.   Include the following intonation patterns:
   • Statement (the voice starts higher and moves downward like going down a staircase through each sound unit in a statement. When the end of the statement is reached, at the period, the voice falls).
   • WH-Questions (the voice begins on a high note with the WH-Question word, then falls through the middle of the sentence until the last content word when the voice rises to accent the accented syllable in the last content word and then falls).

B. Have students complete *To Do Second and To Do Third.* Call on individual students to read the conversation after each substitution has been drilled.

To Do First: Repeat the conversation after the instructor.

Cleaning House

Speaker A: Mother
Speaker B: Children

1.A.   It's time to clean the house. **Mary, wash the dishes.**
   1.B.   Where's the **dish detergent**?
2.A.   The **dish detergent** is **under the sink**.
   2.B.   O.K.
3.A.   **John, do the laundry.**
   3.B.   Where's the **laundry detergent**?
4.A.   The **laundry detergent** is **in the cabinet**.
   4.B.   O.K.

To Do Second: Speak with a partner. Change the underlined words in the conversation for the Substitutons in No. 1 below.

Substitution No. 1

1.A.   It's time to clean the house. **Hiromasa, sweep the floors**.
   1.B.   Where's the **broom?**
2.A.   The **broom is in the closet**.
   2.B.   O.K.
3.A.   **Megumi, take out the trash**.
   3.B.   Where're the **trash bags**?
4.A.   The **trash bags are in the cabinet**.
   4.B.   O.K.

To Do Third: Partners present their conversations for the class.

UNIT 5 – HOUSING - LESSON 3 – CLEANING HOUSE
STUDENT BOOK PAGE 75

Grammar Foundation

A. Introduce the Grammar Foundation by reading information under Imperative Commands.

B. Complete *To Do First* by having students repeat each of the Imperative Commands after the instructor.

C. Complete *To Do Second* by having students repeat the example sentences after the instructor.

D. Demonstrate *To Do Third*.
   1. The instructor gives several Imperative Commands for students to do in the class, for example: "Stand up, walk to the door, pick up your book, or turn off the light."
   2. After sufficient demonstration, students work with a partner and continue the activity in pairs.

Grammar Foundation

To Do First: Read the information about Imperative Commands with the instructor.

To Do Second: Repeat the example sentences after the instructor.

1. Imperative Commands

The Imperative is used to give a command or an instruction. The sentence usually begins with the command. Examples of imperatives for this lesson include: wash, do, sweep, and take out.

Imperatives are used when you want to tell someone to do something such as commands, orders, instructions, or polite requests. In an Imperative sentence, use the base form of the verb. Imperatives are often used without a subject in the sentence. For example:

- Stop!
- Open the door.
- Do the laundry.
- Please take out the garbage.

The negative imperative uses 'Don't'.

- Don't talk to me.
- Don't wash the dishes.
- Don't answer the phone.
- Please don't do that.

When you want someone to do something with you, use 'Let's'.

- Let's go to the park.
- Let's sweep the floors.
- Let's make a long distance phone call.

NOTE: Often an imperative is preceded by the person's name to whom the command or direction is given. For example: John, do the laundry.

To Do Third:
1. Speak with a partner.
2. Student 1 makes an Imperative Command, for example, 'stand up'.

151

UNIT 5 – HOUSING - LESSON 3 – CLEANING HOUSE
STUDENT BOOK PAGE 76

E. Introduce the Grammar Foundation by reading the information about Prepositions of Location.

F. Complete _To Do First_ by having students repeat example sentences after the instructor.

1. G. Complete _To Do Second_ for practice with comprehension of the Prepositions of Location. The instructor will place an object somewhere in the room, for example, place a book on the table.
2. Students respond with a statement about the book which uses a Preposition of Location, for example: "The book is on the table."
3. Use all the Prepositions of Location introduced including under, next to, across from, on, and in.

G. Complete _To Do Third_. Conduct a Question and Answer Chain Drill.
- The instructor places an object somewhere in the room, for example, place a book on the table.
- The instructor asks Student 1: "Where's the book?"
- Student 1 answers: "The book is on the table."
- The instructor moves the object to another place in the room.
- Student 1 asks Student 2: "Where's the book?"
- Student 2 answers.
- Continue until all students have both asked and answered questions.

3. Student 2 performs the action.
4. Student 2 makes an Imperative Command.
5. Student 1 performs the action.

2. Prepositions of Location

To Do First: Read the information about Prepositions of Location. Repeat the example sentences after the instructor.

Prepositions of Location are used to show the relationship of two objects to each other. Some common Prepositions of Location are: in, at, under, above, on, next to, between, across from, etc. Here's the structure:

Noun   + Be + Preposition + Noun

The dish soap	is	under	the sink.
The dryer	is	next to	the washing machine.
The church	is	across from	the supermarket.
The laundry	is	on	the table.
The trash bags	are	under	the sink.
The broom	is	in	the closet.
The dishes	are	in	the dish washer.
The laundry	is	in	the dryer.

To Do Second:
1. The instructor will place an object somewhere in the room, for example, the instructor places a book on the table.
2. Students respond with a statement about the book.
3. Use the correct preposition, for example: "The book is on the table".

To Do Third:
1. The instructor will place an object somewhere in the room, for example, the instructor places a book on the table.
2. The instructor will ask Student 1: "Where's the book?"
3. Student 1 answers: "The book is on the table."
4. The instructor moves the object to another place in the room.
5. Student 1 asks to Student 2: "Where's the book?"
6. Student 2 answers.
7. Continue until all students have asked and answered questions.

UNIT 5 – HOUSING - LESSON 3 – CLEANING HOUSE
STUDENT BOOK PAGE 77

Let's Practice

A. Conduct the Let's Practice Activity 1. Verbs in the Bag
   1. Prepare in advance. Prepare a set of 3x5 index cards with the cleaning commands from the vocabulary, one command per card.
   2. Place the cards into a brown paper bag or other opaque container.
   3. The instructor demonstrates the activity by drawing a card from the bag, reading it silently, and performing the action without speaking.
   4. Students guess what action the instructor is doing.
   5. Continue with each student pantomiming a cleaning action.

B. Conduct the Let's Practice Activity 2. Cleaning Tasks and Products Mix & Match
   1. Prepare in advance. Use the same 3x5 index cards prepared for Verbs in the Bag with cleaning commands from the vocabulary. Prepare a second set of 3x5 index cards with the cleaning products or tools from the vocabulary. Each cleaning command card should have a matching cleaning product or tool card.
   2. Distribute the cards around to the students.
   3. Students walk around to find the match for their cards: cleaning products or tools matched with cleaning commands, for example: 'sweep the floor' matches with 'broom.'

C. Have students complete the Let's Practice Activity 3. House Cleaning Survey
   1. Have students open their books to the activity.
   2. The instructor demonstrates the interview by asking a student, "Who washes the dishes in your house?" Student answers. Write the student's name or the name of his/her family member who washes the dishes.
   3. Students talk to each other to complete their surveys.
   4. Note: guard against students copying each other's books without speaking.

D. Conduct the Let's Practice Activity 4. Every Week We Clean the House – Add On Game
   1. Prepare in advance. Use the same 3x5 index cards for cleaning commands.
   2. Place the cleaning command cards into a brown paper bag.
   3. The instructor demonstrates by drawing a cleaning command card from the bag, for example: 'sweep the floor.'
   4. The instructor makes the statement: "Every week we clean the house. I sweep the floor."
   5. Student 1 takes a card from the bag, for example, 'wash the dishes' and repeats the instructor's statement: "Every week we clean the house. SHE sweeps the floor, and I wash the dishes."
   6. Continue until all students have repeated previous students' responses and added a cleaning command. Students are practicing Third Person Present Tense verb –S endings.

1. Verbs in the Bag
1. Student 1 takes a card from the bag and performs the action without speaking.
2. For example, the card says: sweep the floor. Student 1 pantomimes sweeping the floor. The class guesses what action Student 1 is doing.

2. Cleaning Tasks and Products Mix & Match
1. The instructor will give each student a card. Half of the cards have cleaning tasks, for example: 'sweep the floor'. The other half of the cards will have the cleaning products or tools, for example: 'broom'.
2. Students walk around to find the match for their card.
3. Read matches to the class.

3. House Cleaning Survey
Students talk to each other. Ask: Who does the house cleaning jobs in your family?
Write the student's names under the cleaning jobs.

Name	Dishes	Laundry	Sweeping	Taking out Trash
Barbara	*Barbara*	*Barbara*	*Bernie*	*Bernie*

4. Every Week We Clean the House – Add On Game
1. Student 1 takes a cleaning job card from the bag, for example: 'sweep the floor.'
2. Student 1 makes a sentence, "Every week we clean the house. I sweep the floor."
3. Student 2 takes a card from the bag, for example: 'wash the dishes'.
4. Student 2 repeats Student 1's statement, then adds a statement, for example: "Every week we clean the house. SHE sweeps the floor, and I wash the dishes."
5. Continue until all students have added a cleaning job.

UNIT 5 – HOUSING - LESSON 3 – CLEANING HOUSE
STUDENT BOOK PAGE 78

E. Conduct the Let's Practice Activity 5. The Lost Coin Pantomime
Note this is the biblical principle.

1. Prepare in advance. See Materials and Preparation on the first page of this unit.
2. The instructor hides one of the $1,000 dollar bills somewhere in the room before class begins. Select a student Reader. Ensure the student understands to read only what's under the Reader column and to pause after reading each sentence so the instructor can perform the action.
3. Dim the lights in the room or turn off the lights and use the flash light or lamp.
4. After each line the Reader reads, the instructor performs the action.
5. Complete *To Do Second* by explaining the meaning of the story.

4. Student 2 repeats Student 1's statement, then adds a statement, for example: "Every week we clean the house. HE sweeps the floor, and I wash the dishes."

5. Continue until all students have added a cleaning job.

5. The Lost Coin Pantomime

To Do First:

1. The class chooses one student to be the Reader.
2. The instructor will be the Actor.
3. The Reader reads the sentences. Stop at the end of each sentence so the instructor can perform the actions.

Reader	Instructor
1. A woman had 10 $1,000 dollar bills.	Woman counts her money out loud.
2. She loses 1 of the $1,000 dollar bills.	Woman counts again; only 9 bills.
3. What does she do?	Woman panics.
4. She turns on the light.	Woman turns on the light.
5. She sweeps her house.	Woman sweeps whole house.
6. She looks carefully everywhere.	Woman looks around whole room.
7. She finds the money!	Woman finds the lost money.
8. When she finds it, she calls her friends.	Woman calls friends on cell phone.
9. The woman says:	Woman shouts, "I'm happy! I have found my lost money!"

To Do Second: Listen to the instructor tell the meaning of the story.

UNIT 5 – HOUSING - LESSON 3 – CLEANING HOUSE
STUDENT BOOK PAGE 79

<u>Review Exercises</u>

Assign Review Exercises for homework.

2. <u>Mystery Word Search</u>
1. Go over the instructions for the Mystery Word Search to ensure everyone knows how to complete the activity. Perhaps do the first 2 in class.
2. This is a two-part exercise.
3. Students complete *To Do First* by completing the sentences No. 1-10 using words from the vocabulary.
4. For the second part of the activity, students take their answers to the sentence completions and write the words into the puzzle putting one letter on each line.
5. If students have completed the sentence completions correctly, a mystery word will appear vertically inside the box. The instructor reveals the mystery word in the next class. The mystery word is: Clean House

Answer Key – words in bold

1. My trash bags are in the ***<u>cabinet.</u>***

2. I **<u>do</u> <u>laundry</u>** every week.

3. I use a broom to **<u>sweep</u> <u>the</u> <u>floor</u>**.

4. I **<u>wash</u> <u>dishes</u>** every day.

5. My dish detergent is under the **<u>sink</u>**.

6. I use **___<u>dish</u> <u>detergent</u>** to wash dishes.

7. My **<u>broom</u>** is in the closet.

8. I use **<u>laundry</u> <u>detergent</u>** to wash clothes.

1. Writing

Write 5 sentences about the house cleaning jobs you do each week.

Every week I do the laundry. _____

_____

_____

_____

_____

2. Mystery Word Search

To Do First:

1. Complete the sentences No. 1-10 below.
2. Write the answer from the sentences on the lines in the puzzle with one letter on each line.
3. When finished, a mystery word will appear inside the box.
4. Write the mystery word on the line.

1. My trash bags are in the ***cabinet.***

2. I _____ _____ every week.

3. I use a broom to _____ _____ _____.

4. I _____ _____ every day.

5. My dish detergent is under the _____.

6. I use _____ _____ to wash dishes.

7. My _____ is in the closet.

8. I use _____ _____ to wash clothes.

UNIT 5 – HOUSING - LESSON 3 – CLEANING HOUSE
STUDENT BOOK PAGE 80

9. I use large black **trash bags**.

10. My broom is in the **closet**.

To Do Second: Write the answers to the questions above on the lines below.

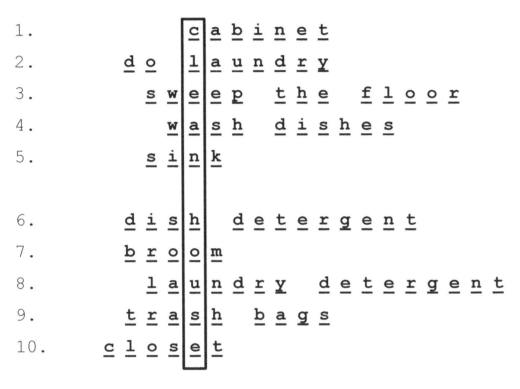

1. c a b i n e t

2. d o l a u n d r y

3. s w e e p t h e f l o o r

4. w a s h d i s h e s

5. s i n k

6. d i s h d e t e r g e n t

7. b r o o m

8. l a u n d r y d e t e r g e n t

9. t r a s h b a g s

10. c l o s e t

To Do Third: Write the mystery word inside the box on the line: clean house.

9. I use large black _____ _____.

10. My broom is in the _____.

To Do Second: Write the answers to the questions above on the lines below.

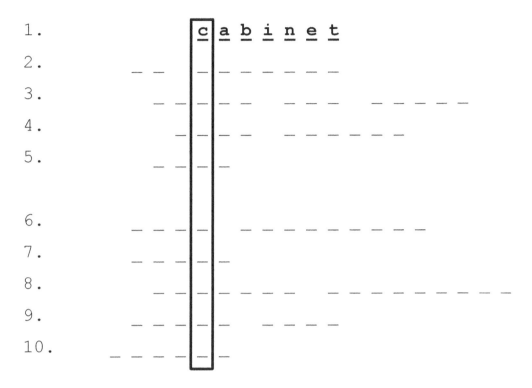

1.

2.

3.

4.

5.

6.

7.

8.

9.

10.

To Do Third: Write the mystery word inside the box on the line: _____.

Look how far you've come! Just a little more to go!

UNIT 6 – MEDICAL - LESSON 1 – THE BODY
STUDENT BOOK PAGE 81

A. Prayer for Students & Self

B. Lesson Objective and Functions:
• Identifying human body parts

C. Grammar Structures:
• Possessive Adjectives

D. Biblical Reference or Principles:
How God Created Man & Woman - Condensed from Genesis 2:7; 15; 18; 19A; 20B; 21-23:
And the Lord God formed man from the dust of the ground and breathed into his nostrils the breath of life, and man became a living being. ... The Lord God took the man and put him in the Garden of Eden to work it and take care of it. . . . The Lord God said, "It is not good for the man to be alone. I will make a helper suitable for him." . . . Now the Lord God had formed out of the ground all the beasts of the field and all the birds of the air. . . . But for Adam no suitable helper was found. So the Lord God caused the man to fall into a deep sleep; and while he was sleeping, he took one of the man's ribs and closed up the place with flesh. Then the Lord God made a woman from the rib he had taken out of the man, and he brought her to the man. The man said, "This is now bone of my bones and flesh of my flesh; and she shall be called 'woman,' for she was taken out of man."

E. Materials & Preparation:
   1. For the activity The Five Senses Concentration, prepare a Concentration game board. See instructions in the Activity Bank. Prepare the Concentration game cards. Five cards have one each of the five senses while the other 5 cards have the matching body part, for example, 'nose' and 'smell'. Also a ball or soft object to throw is needed.
   2. For the activity Body Parts Line Up, prepare a set of 3x5 index cards with one each of the 16 body parts from the vocabulary.

Introduction
   1. Conduct a Listing activity. The instructor asks: "Who can name a part of the body?" Write whatever body parts the s tudents name on the board.
   2. Say: "Today we are going to learn the diffeent parts of the body."

Introduce New Vocabulary
   1. Have students open to Unit 6 – Medical; Lesson 1 – The Body.
   2. Using the body drawing, introduce the parts of the body with a repetition drill.
   3. After every 4 words introduced, review.

UNIT 6 - MEDICAL
LESSON 1 – THE BODY

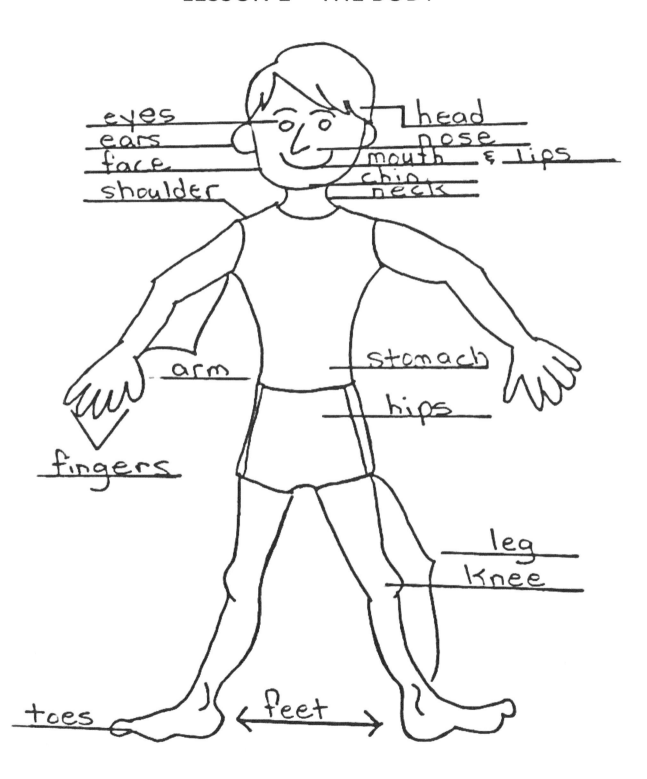

UNIT 6 – MEDICAL - LESSON 1 – THE BODY
STUDENT BOOK PAGE 82

Time to Speak

A. Complete *To Do First:*
   1. Introduce the conversation under Time to Speak. Have students repeat each line after the instructor. Repeat each line 5-6 times. Strive for a normal, conversation tone rather than an oral reading tone.
   2. Use backward build up for sentences longer than 4 words. Remember to divide sentences into their sound units.
   3. Use correct intonation, stress, and rhythm patterns. Include the following intonation patterns:
   - Statement (the voice starts higher and moves downward like going down a staircase through each sound unit in a statement. When the end of the statement is reached, at the period, the voice falls).
   - WH-Questions (the voice begins on a high note with the WH-Question word, then falls through the middle of the sentence until the last content word when the voice rises to accent the accented syllable in the last content word and then falls).

B. Have students complete *To Do Second.* Try spelling one of the words with in a chanting manner to keep interest.

C. Have students complete *To Do Third.* Call on student pairs to perform the conversation for the class.

Practicing Perfect Pronunciation

   1. Have students practice pronunciation of the word pairs by repeating 5-6 times after the instructor.
   2. Volunteers present for the class.

eyes / ears   legs / lips   tummy / toes   chin / cheeks   hips / lips

To Do First: Repeat the conversation after the instructor. Touch each of your body parts as you say them.

The Body

Speaker A - Parent
Speaker B - Child

1.A. Hi Johnny. What did you learn in school today?
   1.B. I learned the parts of the body.
2.A. Great! Show me the parts of the body.
   2.B. O.K. We learned them with a chant. Say it after me.
   My feet, my tummy, my arms, my chin.
3.A. My feet, my tummy, my arms, my chin.
   3.B. My legs, my lips, my hips, my cheeks.
4.A. My legs, my lips, my hips, my cheeks.
   4.B. My eyes, my ears, my mouth, my nose.
5.A. My eyes, my ears, my mouth, my nose.
   5.B. My head, my shoulders, my knees, my toes.
6.A. My head, my shoulders, my knees, my toes.
That's great, Johnny!

To Do Second: Spell the parts of the body after the instructor.

To Do Third: Work with a partner. Student 1 says one of the body parts. Student 2 touches his/her body part. Student 2 says one of the body parts. Student 1 touches his/her body part. Continue with all 16 parts of the body.

~~ Practicing Perfect Pronunciation ~~

Repeat each pair of words after the instructor:

eyes / ears   legs / lips   tummy / toes   chin / cheeks   hips / lips

UNIT 6 – MEDICAL – LESSON 1 – THE BODY
STUDENT BOOK PAGE 83

Grammar Foundation

A. Introduce the Grammar Foundation by reading the information and example sentences under Possessive Adjectives.

B. Complete *To Do First* by having students repeat each example sentence after the instructor.

C. Complete *To Do Second* by having the students repeat the Pronouns and Possessive Adjectives after the instructor.

D. Complete *To Do Third*. The instructor will write the Pronouns on the board.
The instructor will hold up a book and point to one of the Pronouns on the board, for example, 'I'. Students will answer with the correct Possessive Adjective, for example, "my book."

E. For *To Do Fourth* have students complete the sentences using the Possessive Adjectives. Go over student responses.

Answer Key – in bold
1. I am sick. **My** tummy hurts.
2. John broke **his** arm yesterday.
3. My cat got **its** tail caught in the door.
4. Johnny put on **his** shoes.
5. My grandparents wear glasses. **Their** eyes are bad.

Continued next page…

Continued next page…

NOTE to the instructor: Here's something interesting for you to work out. How would you complete these two sentences?
   1. Johnny, put on ____ shoes.
   2. Johnny put on ____ shoes.
The inclusion of the comma in sentence 1 changes the statement into an Imperative Command and the only correct completion would be **your.**
Sentence 2, on the other hand, would be completed with the Possessive Adjective.

Grammar Foundation

Possessive Adjectives

Use a Possessive Adjective before a Noun to show who the Noun belongs to. For example:

My mother.	Meaning: mother belongs to me. She is my mother.
My head.	Meaning: this head belongs to me. It is my head.
My house.	Meaning: this house belongs to me. I own this house. It's my house.
My children.	Meaning: the children belong to me. They're my children.
My father.	Meaning: father belongs to me. He's my father.

To Do First: Repeat the sentences after the instructor.

To Do Second: Repeat the Possessive Adjectives after the instructor.

Here's a chart of all the Possessive Adjectives:

Pronoun	Possessive Adjective	Pronoun	Possessive Adjective
I	my	it	its
you	your	we	our
she	her	you	your
he	his	they	their

To Do Third: Practice the Possessive Adjectives.
1. The instructor will write the Pronouns on the board.
2. The instructor will hold up a book and point to one of the Pronouns on the board.
3. Students will answer with the correct Possessive Adjective. For example, if the instructor points to the Pronoun 'I', students will answer with the Possessive Adjective 'my' book.

To Do Fourth: Complete the Possessive Adjective sentences below.

1. I am sick. __**My**__ tummy hurts.
2. John broke _____ arm yesterday.
3. My cat got _____ tail caught in the door.
4. Johnny put on _____ shoes.
5. My grandparents wear glasses. _____ eyes are bad.

UNIT 6 – MEDICAL – LESSON 1 – THE BODY
STUDENT BOOK PAGE 84

6. Jane wears a hearing aid. **Her** ears are bad.
7. Mom and Dad, here are **your** keys.
8. We are going to the dentist. We have to get **our** teeth cleaned.

Let's Practice

A. Conduct the Let's Practice Activity 1. Simon Says
    1. Have all students stand up.
    2. The instructor is 'Simon'.
    3. Simon gives a command, for example: "Simon says touch your nose." All students touch their noses.
    4. If Simon gives a command and does NOT say "Simon says...", students should NOT perform the action. If a student performs the action when Simon did not say "Simon says..." that student is out and must sit down.
    5. The last student standing is the winner.
    6. After several rounds, ask for a volunteer to be Simon.

B. Conduct the Let's Practice Activity 2. The Five Senses Concentration
    1. Complete *To Do First* by having the students repeat each sense after the instructor. Repeat each one 5-6 times with a repetition drill.
    2. Complete *To Do Second* by introducing the five senses with the corresponding body part. Teach each pair with a repetition drill 5-6 times each.
    3. Complete *To Do Third*.
    4. The instructor says one of the senses and throws a soft ball to Student 1.
    5. Student 1 catches the ball and says the corresponding body part. For example, the instructor says, "smell" and throws the ball. The student responds with "nose". Student 1 throws the ball back to the instructor. Continue until all students have practiced matching senses and body parts.
    6. Complete *To Do Fourth* by playing Five Senses Concentration.
    7. Prepare in advance. Create a Concentration game board following the instructions in the Activity Bank. Prepare 10 3x5 index cards for the Concentration board. On five cards put one each of the 5 senses and on the other 5 cards, one each of the corresponding body parts. For example: see -- eyes.
    8. To play, see the Activity Bank for directions.

6. Jane wears a hearing aid. _____ ears are bad.

7. Mom and Dad, here are _____ keys.

8. We are going to the dentist. We have to get _____ teeth cleaned.

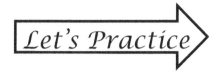

Let's Practice

1. Simon Says

1. The instructor is 'Simon'.

2. Simon gives a command. Students respond. For example: "Simon says touch your nose." All students touch their noses.

3. If Simon gives a command and does NOT say "Simon says…", students should NOT perform the action. For example, the instructor says: "Touch your nose." Students should NOT perform the action.

4. If a student performs the action when the instructor does NOT say "Simon says…", that student is out and must sit down. The last student standing is the winner.

2. The Five Senses Concentration

To Do First: Learn the five senses: Taste, touch, hear, smell, see.

Repeat each sense after the instructor.

To Do Second: Match the five senses with the body part:

taste – mouth   touch – hands   hear – ears   smell – nose   see – eyes

Repeat each sense and body part after the instructor.

To Do Third: Practice the five senses and the body part.

1. The instructor will say one of the senses and throw a ball.

2. Student 1 catches the ball and says the body part. For example, the instructor says, "smell" and throws the ball. Student 1 catches the ball and says, "nose".

3. Student 1 throws the ball to the instructor.

To Do Fourth: Play Five Senses Concentration

1. Work with a partner or work with the whole class.

2. In the Concentration board are 10 cards. Five cards have senses and 5 cards have body parts.

3. Student 1 chooses 2 cards from the Concentration board and reads them to the class. For example: 'nose' and 'smell'. These 2 cards match – the body part and the correct sense. Cards are removed from the board and Student 1 receives one point.

4. Student 2 chooses 2 cards and reads them to the class. For example: 'eyes' and 'ears'. These 2 cards do NOT match – they are both body parts. Student 2 puts these cards back into the board.

5. Continue until all cards are matched and removed from the board.

UNIT 6 – MEDICAL – LESSON 1 – THE BODY
STUDENT BOOK PAGE 85

C. Conduct the Let's Practice Activity 3. Body Parts Line Up

1. Prepare in advance. Create sets of 16 index cards with one each of the 16 body parts. Prepare enough sets for several small groups of students.
2. Give each group a set of cards.
3. Groups work together to put the cards into alphabetical order (A-Z).
4. Students read their cards in order to the class.

D. Conduct the Let's Practice Activity 4. What Can The Body Do? – Group Brainstorm Activity

1. Write one of the body parts on the board. For example: eyes.
2. Ask: "What can eyes do?" Write all the things eyes can do on the board. For example: see, blink, squint, cry, etc.
3. Have students work in pairs or small groups. Assign one of the remaining body parts to each group, for example: foot, arm, hand, etc. Groups write a list of all the actions their body part can do.
4. Groups read their lists to the class.

E. Conduct the Let's Practice Activity 5. How God Created Man and Woman
Note this is the biblical principle.

1. Read the story, below, to the students while they follow along silently.
   Genesis 2:7; 15; 18; 19A; 20B; 21-23: And the Lord God formed man from the dust of the ground and breathed into his nostrils the breath of life, and man became a living being. . . . The Lord God took the man and put him in the Garden of Eden to work it and take care of it. . . . The Lord God said, "It is not good for the man to be alone. I will make a helper suitable for him." . . . Now the Lord God had formed out of the ground all the beasts of the field and all the birds of the air. . . . But for Adam no suitable helper was found. So the Lord God caused the man to fall into a deep sleep; and while he was sleeping, he took one of the man's ribs and closed up the place with flesh. Then the Lord God made a woman from the rib he had taken out of the man, and he brought her to the man. The man said, "This is now bone of my bones and flesh of my flesh; and she shall be called 'woman,' for she was taken out of man."
2. Complete *To Do Second* by having students close their books.
3. Use the 8 ½ x 11 pictures following this lesson to present the Lipson style story: "How God Created Man and Woman". For general instructions on the Lipson method, see Activity Bank.
4. Use the full sized pictures to drill each sentence of the story with a repetition drill and backward build up. Repeat each sentence 5-6 times.
5. Have students complete *To Do Third*. After all sentences have been drilled, ask for student volunteers to retell the story using the instructor's pictures as prompts. Instructor may wish to photocopy pictures and place on board. Alternately, students can turn to Activity 3 in their Review Exercises to see the pictures.

3. Body Parts Line Up

1. Work with a small group. The instructor will give each group a set of cards with the body parts.
2. Group works together to put the cards into alphabetical order A-Z.
3. Students read their cards to the class.

4. What Can The Body Do? - Group Brainstorm Activity

1. Work with a partner. The instructor will give you one of the body parts, for example, the foot.
2. Write a list of all the actions the foot can do, for example: walk, stand…
3. Read your list to the class.

5. How God Created Man and Woman

Here's the story from the Scriptures about how God created man and woman. Later, you can read the whole story in Genesis 2:7-25.

To Do First: Listen to the instructor read the story. Follow along silently.

Genesis 2:7; 15; 18; 19A; 20B; 21-23:

And the Lord God formed man from the dust of the ground and breathed into his nostrils the breath of life, and man became a living being. . . . The Lord God took the man and put him in the Garden of Eden to work it and take care of it. . . . The Lord God said, "It is not good for the man to be alone. I will make a helper suitable for him." . . . Now the Lord God had formed out of the ground all the beasts of the field and all the birds of the air. . . . But for Adam no suitable helper was found. So the Lord God caused the man to fall into a deep sleep; and while he was sleeping, he took one of the man's ribs and closed up the place with flesh. Then the Lord God made a woman from the rib he had taken out of the man, and he brought her to the man. The man said, "This is now bone of my bones and flesh of my flesh; and she shall be called 'woman,' for she was taken out of man."

To Do Second: Close your books. Repeat each sentence after the instructor.

To Do Third:

1. Use the instructor's pictures or see the pictures in Activity 3 Review Exercises.
2. Tell the story to your partner.
3. Volunteers can tell the story to the class.

UNIT 6 – MEDICAL – LESSON 1 – THE BODY
STUDENT BOOK PAGE 86

Review Exercises

Assign Review Exercises for homework. Go over the instructions to ensure students know how to complete the activities.

1. Hidden Body Parts and Senses

Answer Key – words in bold

TUMMY	ARMS	FEET	CHIN	SEEING	TOUCH
LEGS	LIPS	HIPS	CHEEKS	HEARING	BODY
EYES	EARS	MOUTH	NOSE	TASTE	
HEAD	SHOULDERS	KNEES	TOES	SMELL	

```
A R M S N K L H F D S C H I N A K N Q I Y B O D Y N A S
A N I Y T O U C H N E W Q H N S B Q W E R T U M M Y W E
F N A E T Y F E E T G H J K O I U Y T S E E I N G W T E
N I Y N E W S M E L L E R T H E A D Y I O W Q E T O E S
Q W E R T Q W E R T T H E A D H I O E T R Q W H E H K E
N T R E Q Y I O P B V C S H O U L D E R S H Q T I Y I E
K K N E E S S B M A B J I Y K L E G S S N I Y Q E E B Q
N T H E A R I N G N H L I H H H I P S S Q W E R T T Y I
N L L I P S S N Y I Q W E R T N M N O B V Q W E A R S G
N K F D S C H E E K S N K L Q W D E R F T T G N K L P O
N O S E Q N H K N L E A R S N I Y E Y E S S E Y N O O S
Q W E R T Y N M O U T H B N M T A S T E B J K H G F D S
```

2. Complete the Sentences
1. I use my **mouth** to taste and eat.
2. I use my **nose** to smell.
3. I use my **hands** to touch.
4. I use my **eyes** to see.
5. I use my **ears** to hear.

Review Exercises

1. Hidden Body Parts and Senses

Circle the body parts and senses in the puzzle.

TUMMY	ARMS	FEET	CHIN	SEEING	TOUCH
LEGS	LIPS	HIPS	CHEEKS	HEARING	BODY
EYES	EARS	MOUTH	NOSE	TASTE	HEAD
KNEES	TOES	SHOULDERS	SMELL		

```
A R M S N K L H F D S C H I N A K N Q I Y B O D Y N A S
A N I Y T O U C H N E W Q H N S B Q W E R T U M M Y W E
F N A E T Y F E E T G H J K O I U Y T S E E I N G W T E
N I Y N E W S M E L L E R T H E A D Y I O W Q E T O E S
Q W E R T Q W E R T T H E A D H I O E T R Q W H E H K E
N T R E Q Y I O P B V C S H O U L D E R S H Q T I Y I E
K K N E E S S B M A B J I Y K L E G S S N I Y Q E E B Q
N T H E A R I N G N H L I H H H I P S S Q W E R T T Y I
N L L I P S S N Y I Q W E R T N M N O B V Q W D A S D G
N K F D S C H E E K S N K L Q W D E R F T T G N K L P O
N O S E Q N H K N L E A R S N I Y E Y E S S E Y N O O S
Q W E R T Y N M O U T H B N M T A S T E B J K H G F D S
```

2. Complete the Sentences

1. I use my   ___*mouth*___   to taste and eat.

2. I use my _____ to smell.

3. I use my _____ to touch.

4. I use my_____ to see.

5. I use my _____ to hear.

UNIT 6 – MEDICAL – LESSON 1 – THE BODY
STUDENT BOOK PAGE 87

3. Write the Story: How God Created Man and Woman

1. Below you will see the pictures for the story How God Created Man and Woman.
2. Write a sentence for each picture to tell the story.

3. Write the Story: How God Created Man and Woman

1. Below you will see the pictures for the story How God Created Man and Woman.
2. Write a sentence for each picture to tell the story.

1.

2.

3.

4.& 5.

6.& 7.

1. _____
2. _____
3. _____
4. _____
5. _____
6. _____
7. _____

UNIT 6 – MEDICAL – LESSON 1 – THE BODY

Story Sentences	Picture Descriptions
1. God made man from dust.	Clouds with "God", man on earth.
2. God put man in the garden.	Man in the garden.
3. Man was lonely.	Man with animals; man unhappy.
4. God made man go to sleep.	Man sleeping in bed.
5. God took one of man's ribs.	Man sleeping; rib.
6. God made woman from man's rib.	Woman with rib inside.
7. Man liked woman.	Man smiling at woman.

UNIT 6 – MEDICAL - LESSON 2 – PERSONAL HYGIENE
STUDENT BOOK PAGE 88

A. Prayer for Students & Self

B. Lesson Objective and Functions:
- Describing daily personal hygiene actions

C. Grammar Structures:
- Simple Present Tense
- Present Proressive Tense

D. Biblical Reference or Principles:
- Be clean before God.

E. Materials & Preparation:
- For the activity Personal Hygiene Actions in the Bag Pantomime prepare a set of 5x7 index cards with one each of the personal hygiene actions from the conversation. Also need a brown paper bag or other opaque container.
- For the activity Personal Hygiene Actions Concentration prepare a Concentration game board. See Activity Bank for instructions. Prepare a set of 3x5 index cards with one each with the personal hygiene actions split, for example: card 1 says 'brush' while its match, card 2, says 'my teeth.'

Introduction
1. Do a semantic web in the form of a list.
2. Ask students to name or pantomime personal hygiene actions they do every day such as brushing teeth, shaving, etc.
3. List their responses on the board in columns according to actions a male would do, actions a female would do, and actions that both male and female would do. DO NOT label the columns yet. When finished, read the columns.
4. Ask students to guess which column is Male Actions, which Female Actions, and which Both Male & Female Actions.
5. Students come to board and label the columns as they think.
6. Say: "Tonight we are going to talk about Personal Hygiene practices in the United States."

Introduce New Vocabulary
1. Have students open to Unit 6 – Medical; Lesson 2 – Personal Hygiene.
2. Introduce the 4 hygiene actions using a repetition drill.

Unit 6 - Medical
LESSON 2 – PERSONAL HYGIENE

Above: brush my teeth
Right: comb my hair
Below: wash my face
Below Right: put on deodorant

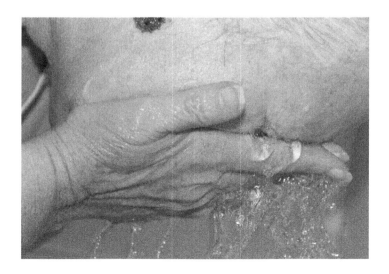

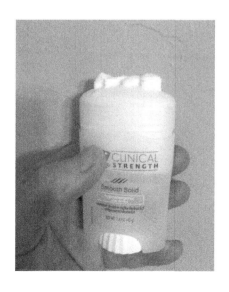

UNIT 6 – MEDICAL - LESSON 2 – PERSONAL HYGIENE
STUDENT BOOK PAGE 89

Continue introducing vocabulary with a Repetition Drill.

take a shower

shampoo my hair

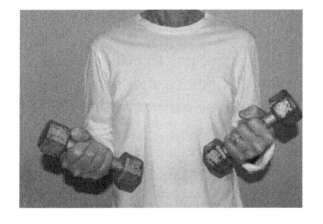

do exercise

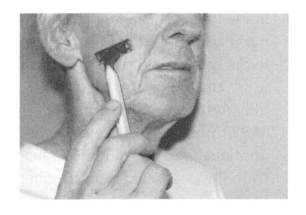

shave my face

UNIT 6 – MEDICAL - LESSON 2 – PERSONAL HYGIENE
STUDENT BOOK PAGE 90

Time to Speak

A. Complete *To Do First:*
1. Introduce the conversation under Time to Speak. Have students repeat each line after the instructor. Repeat each line 5-6 times. Strive for a normal, conversation tone rather than an oral reading tone.
2. Use backward build up for sentences longer than 4 words. Remember to divide sentences into their sound units.
3. Use correct intonation, stress, and rhythm patterns. Include the following intonation patterns:
- Joining Two Actions with AND: raise the voice on the first part of the pair, for example, "brush my teeth", lower the voice for "and", then raise it for the second part of the pair, for example, "wash my face."
- WH-Questions (the voice begins on a high note with the WH-Question word, then falls through the middle of the sentence until the last content word when the voice rises to accent the accented syllable in the last content word and then falls).

B. Have students complete *To Do Second.* Call on individual students to read the conversation after each substitution has been drilled.

C. Have students complete *To Do Third.* This activity is called Pair, Square, Share. It's a two-part activity.
1. In the first part, student pairs interview each other asking, "What do you do every morning?"
2. In the second part, each pair of students joins another pair to make a group of four. The original partners of the group now share their partner's responses to the question with the group of four, for example: "My partner washes her face and brushes her teeth every morning."
3. Continue until all 4 students have introduced their original partners.
4. Note this practices use of the Simple Present Tense third person –s endings on the verb.
5. Place students in pairs.
6. The instructor demonstrates each part of the activity.

My Daily Routine

To Do First: Repeat each sentence after the instructor.

1.A.   Every morning I **brush my teeth** and **wash my face.**
    1.B.   What does your **husband** do?
2.A.   **He shaves his face** and **takes a shower**.
    2.B.   What do you do in the evening?
3.A.   In the evening I **take a shower** and **shampoo my hair.**

To Do Second: Speak with a partner. Change the underlined words in the conversation for the Substitutions in No. 1-2 below.

Substitution No. 1
1.A.   **do exercise** and **comb my hair**
    1.B.   **brother**
2.A.   **washes his face** and **puts on deodorant**
3.A.   **comb my hair** and **put on deodorant**

Substitution No. 2
1.A.   **shampoo my hair** and **comb my hair**
    1.B.   **son**
2.A.   **He does exercise** and **brushes his teeth**
3.A.   **put on deodorant** and **brush my teeth**

To Do Third:
1. Talk with your partner.
2. Student 1 asks: "What do you do every morning?" Student 2 answers.
3. Student 2 asks the question and Student 1 answers.
4. Join with another pair of students. Student 1 tells the group what Student 2 does, for example: "My partner washes his face and brushes his teeth in the morning."
5. Continue until all students have introduced their partners to the group.

UNIT 6 – MEDICAL - LESSON 2 – PERSONAL HYGIENE
STUDENT BOOK PAGE 91

Grammar Foundation

A. Introduce the Grammar Foundation by reading information under Simple Present Tense.

B. Complete _To Do Second_ by having students repeat each example sentence. Point out that third person verbs have –S on the end. Give extra practice with this.

Grammar Foundation

1. Simple Present Tense

Simple Present Tense is used to describe habits and usual activities done every day or regularly.

Use SIMPLE PRESENT TENSE in three ways:

(1) For habits and usual activities such as activities done every day or regularly.
   For example: I get up at 6:00 a.m. every day. I take a vacation every summer.
(2) For timeless facts or truth, generalizations.
   For example: The sun rises in the morning. The Spinach Salad recipe calls for spinach.
(3) For long term or permanent situations.
   For example: I live in Hollywood. My husbands works at the telephone company.

To Do First: Read the information about Simple Present Tense.

Affirmative Statements

Subject + Verb

I	brush	my teeth every day.
You	comb	your hair every morning.
He	shaves*	every night.
She	does*	exercises every day.
It	rains*	every June.
We	go	to church every Sunday.
They	eat	dinner every evening.

* Remember to put the final -s on the end of third person verbs

To Do Second: Repeat the example sentences after the instructor.

UNIT 6 – MEDICAL - LESSON 2 – PERSONAL HYGIENE
STUDENT BOOK PAGE 92

A. Introduce the Grammar Foundation by reading information under Present Progressive Tense.

B. Complete *To Do Second* by having students repeat each example sentence after the instructor.

C. Ask students to make additional 'ing ending sentences.

Practicing Perfect Pronunciation

Pronouncing –S Endings
Many English language learners have difficulty with –S endings, particularly in pronouncing the Voiced –S ending /z/ sounds. The instructor can help students 'discover' how to vibrate their voice boxes to produce the /z/ sounds which are so common in spoken English particularly in Third Person Present Tense verbs.
1. Introduce the information about Voiced and Voiceless sounds.
The instructor should demonstrate feeling his/her voice box while producing the Voiced words of shave, comb, shampoo, and do.
2. Demonstrate producing the Voiceless ending words of take and put, both of which end in the Voiceless sounds of /k/ and /t/.
To help students shift between the /s/ and /z/ sounds, alternate between the sound of "shhh, be quiet" /s/ sound, and the buzzing bee /z/ sound. Lead student to practice this shift of sounds.

2. Present Progressive Tense

Present Progressive Tense is also known as Present Continuous Tense. We use the Present Progressive Tense to describe action that is happening at the present moment. It is continuous action. It is action that is happening while the speaker is speaking. Here's the grammar structure:

To Do First: Read the information about Present Progressive Tense.

Affirmative Statements

Subject + Be Verb + Main Verb + 'Ing Ending

Singular Forms

I	am	brushing	my teeth.
You	are	combing	your hair.
She	is	taking	a shower.
He	is	putting on	deodorant.

Plural Forms

We	are	doing	exercises.
You	are	watching	T.V.
They	are	shaving	their faces.

To Do Second: Repeat the example sentences after the instructor.

~~ *Practicing Perfect Pronunciation* ~~

Pronouncing -S Endings

1. Sounds are either Voiced or Voiceless For Voiced sounds, you use your voice box to vibrate the sound – for example, say: "shave, comb, shampoo." For Voiceless Sounds, your voice box does not vibrate – for example, say: "take, put."

2. Nouns ending in –S are pronounced with 3 different sounds. Feel your voice box. Put your hands on your throat. Say the Voiced words: "shave, comb, shampoo, do." Can you feel the voice box vibrating on the end of each word? Now pronounce some Voiceless words. Put your hand on your voice box and say these

UNIT 6 – MEDICAL - LESSON 2 – PERSONAL HYGIENE
STUDENT BOOK PAGE 93

3. Read the information under 3. The last group of –S ending words. These words are produced by adding an extra syllable on the end of the word. The words in this group all end with either –SH; -CH; -SS; or –X. Pronounce the following:

SH – wash – washes   CH – teach – teaches   SS – kiss – kisses   X – fix - fixes

Let's Practice

A. Conduct the Let's Practice Activity 1. Personal Hygiene Actions in the Bag Pantomime.
   1. Prepare in advance. Create a set of 3x5 cards with one each of the personal hygiene actions from the conversation, for example: 'brush my teeth.' Place the cards into a brown paper bag or other opaque container.
   2. The instructor demonstrates by drawing a card from the bag, for example, 'brush my teeth' and performing the action without speaking. Ask students, "What am I doing?" Students respond, "You are brushing your teeth."
   3. Have students take cards from the bag and perform the action while the class guesses the action.
   4. Continue until all students have performed a personal hygiene action.

B. Conduct the Let's Practice Activity 2. Personal Hygiene Actions Concentration.
   1. Prepare in advance. Create a Concentration game board following the instructions in the Activity Bank.
   2. Prepare 3x5 index cards for the Concentration board. On half of the cards put one half of a personal hygiene action, for example, 'brush'. On the other half of the cards put the other half of the personal hygiene actions, for example, 'my teeth.'
   3. To play Concentration, see instructions in the Activity Bank.

words: "take, put." There's no vibration of the voice box. So, here's how to pronounce –S endings correctly:

- Voiced Ending Sounds   Make a /z/ sound like a buzzing bee
- Voiceless Ending Sounds   Make an /s/ sound like "shhh, be quiet"

3. The last group of –S ending words are pronounced with an extra syllable on the end of the word. Verbs that are spelled at the end with –SH; -CH; -SS; -X, for example: -SH – wash; CH – teach; SS – kiss; X – fix – add an extra syllable to the end of the word. The instructor will help you hear this pronunciation.

1. Personal Hygiene Actions in the Bag Pantomime
1. Student 1 takes a card with a personal hygiene action from the bag and performs the action without speaking.
2. The class guesses which action Student 1 is performing, for example: "You are brushing your teeth."
3. Student 2 takes a card and performs the action.
4. Continue until all students have performed a personal hygiene action.

2. Personal Hygiene Actions Concentration
1. Work with a partner or work with the whole class. In the Concentration board are some cards. Half the cards have half of a personal hygiene action, for example: 'brush'. The other cards have the other half of the personal hygiene action for example: 'my teeth'. Student 1 chooses 2 cards from the Concentration board and reads them to the class. For example: "brush" and "my teeth". These 2 cards match – the complete personal hygiene action. Cards are removed from the board and Student 1 receives one point.
2. Student 2 chooses 2 cards and reads them to the class. For example: "brush" and "wash". These 2 cards do NOT match – they are both the first half of two different personal hygiene actions. Student 2 puts these cards back into the board.
3. Continue until all cards are matched and removed from the board.

UNIT 6 – MEDICAL - LESSON 2 – PERSONAL HYGIENE
STUDENT BOOK PAGE 94

C. Conduct the Let's Practice Activity 3. Personal Hygiene Actions Survey.
1. Have students open their books to the activity.
2. Instructor demonstrates by interviewing one student. Ask the question: "What personal hygiene actions do you do every day?" Write the student's responses on the survey in the book.
3. Direct students to walk around and speak to their classmates.
4. Guard against students simply copying each other's papers rather than speaking to individual students for responses.

D. Conduct the Let's Practice Activity 4. Play Beat the Cat. Note this is the biblical principle.
Prepare the puzzle using the following puzzle sentence: "Be clean before God means to ask God to forgive your sins." See Activity Bank for instructions on how to prepare and play Beat the Cat.

Review Exercises

Assign Review Exercises for homework. Go over the instructions for each activity to ensure students understand how to complete the activities.

1. Listing Personal Hygiene Actions

Answer Key – in bold

See next page …

3. Personal Hygiene Actions Survey

1. Speak to your classmates.
2. Ask the question: "What personal hygiene actions do you do every day? "
3. Write your classmates' answers on your survey.

Name   Question: What personal hygiene actions do you do every day?

Barbara   *She washes her face and brushes her teeth.*

_____

_____

_____

_____

4. Play Beat the Cat

1. This game is like the TV show Wheel of Fortune. The instructor will put a puzzle on the board.
2. Students take turns guessing consonants.
3. If the consonant is in the puzzle, the instructor will write it on the line. If the consonant is NOT in the puzzle, the instructor will draw part of a cat.
4. Continue until only vowels are left in the puzzle.

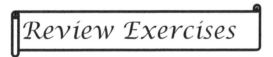

Review Exercises

1. Listing Personal Hygiene Actions

1. Read the personal hygiene actions.
2. Write each action a man does below under the column "Actions for Man", and each action a woman does unde the column "Actions for Woman".
3. Write actions that both man and woman do under the column "Actions for Man & Woman".
4. Add some of your own personal hygiene actions.

UNIT 6 – MEDICAL - LESSON 2 – PERSONAL HYGIENE
STUDENT BOOK PAGE 95

Personal Hygiene Actions

1. wash my face
2. comb my hair
3. brush my teeth
4. put on deodorant

5. shave my face
6. do exercise
7. shampoo my hair
8. take a shower

Actions for Man	Actions for Woman	Actions for Man & Woman
shave my face	wash my face	wash my face
wash my face	comb my hair	comb my hair
comb my hair	brush my teeth	brush my teeth
brush my teeth	put on deodorant	put on deodorant
put on deodorant	do exercise	do exercise
do exercise	shampoo my hair	shampoo my hair
shampoo my hair	take a shower	take a shower
take a shower		

2. Simple Present Tense Vs. Present Progressive Tense

Answer Key – answers in bold

1. [brush] I ___**brush**___ my teeth every morning.

2. [shave] My husband **is shaving** his face right now.

3. [do] We ___**do**___ our exercises after work every day.

4. [take] My son ___**is taking**___ a shower now.

5. [put on] I always ___**put on**___ deodorant in the morning.

6. [shampoo] I never ___**shampoo**___ my hair at night.

7. [wash] Do you **wash** your face every night?

8. [brush] Sorry I didn't answer the phone when you called. I was **brushing** my teeth.

Personal Hygiene Actions

1. wash my face
2. comb my hair
3. brush my teeth
4. put on deodorant

5. shave my face
6. do exercise
7. shampoo my hair
8. take a shower

Actions for Man	Actions for Woman	Actions for Man & Woman
shave my face		*wash my face*

2. Simple Present Tense Vs. Present Progressive Tense

Complete the sentences with the correct form of the Verb in [brackets]. Use Simple Present Tense or Present Progressive Tense.

1. [brush] I __*brush*__ my teeth every morning.

2. [shave] My husband _____ his face right now.

3. [do] We _____ our exercises after work every day.

4. [take]   My son _____a shower now.

5. [put on] I always _____ deodorant in the morning.

6. [shampoo] I never _____my hair at night.

7. [wash] Do you _____ your face every night?

8. [brush] Sorry I didn't answer the phone when you called. I was _____ my teeth.

UNIT 6 – MEDICAL - LESSON 3 – AT THE PHARMACY
STUDENT BOOK PAGE 96

A. Prayer for Students & Self

B. Lesson Objective and Functions:
- Describing common physical ailments
- Identifying appropriate OTC medicines for specific physical ailments

C. Grammar Structures:
- Using Can and Can't; Could and Couldn't
- Using HAVE to Describe Physical Ailments

D. Biblical Reference or Principles:
  - Jesus Healing the Blind Man with Spit Mark 8:22-25:
They came to Bethsaida, and some people brought a blind man and begged Jesus to touch him. He took the blind man by the hand and led him outside the village. When he had spit on the man's eyes and put his hands on him, Jesus asked, "Do you see anything?" He looked up and said, "I see people; they look like trees walking around." Once more Jesus put his hands on the man's eyes. Then his eyes were opened, his sight was restored, and he saw everything clearly.

E. Materials & Preparation:
  - For the activity Medicine Mixer, prepare a set of 3x5 index cards. Half of the cards should have the illnesses from the conversation, for example, 'I have a cold," while the other half of the cards will have the medicines, for example: 'You can take cold medicine.'
  - For the Activity At the Pharmacy Role Play, prepare by gathering a variety of OTC medicines. Alternately, copy the the medicine bottle template located on the Grammar Foundation page and write the medicine names on the bottles, for example, 'aspirin'. Use tacky tape or blue painter's tape to affix the bottles to the board.

Introduction
  1. Say: "When I get a cold, the first thing I do ..." The instructor tells what home remedies or OTC medicines he/she takes for the various illnesses presented in the conversation.
  2. Ask: "What do you do when you are sick? Do you take medicine? Do you go to a doctor?" [get student responses.
  3. Say: "Today we are going to talk about illnesses and medicines we can take for our illnesses."

Introduce New Vocabulary
  1. Have students open to Unit 6 – Medical; Lesson 3 – Medicine
  2. Introduce the 4 illnesses using a repetition drill.
  3. Ask students to pantomime each illness, for example, sneezing, holding the head for a headache, etc.

Unit 6 – Medical
LESSON 3 – AT THE PHARMACY

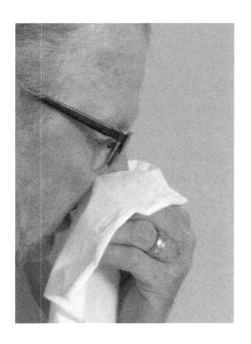

I have a cold.

I have a headache.

I have a sorethroat.

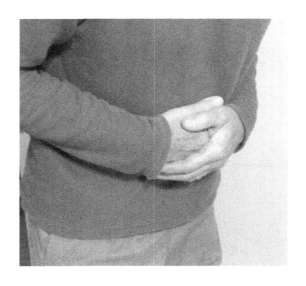

I have a stomachache.

UNIT 6 – MEDICAL - LESSON 3 – AT THE PHARMACY
STUDENT BOOK PAGE 97

1. Continue introducing the vocabulary OTC medicines, pharmacy, and pharmacist using a repetition drill. Repeat each word 5-6 times.
2. Explain the term OTC means 'over the counter' medicine. No prescription is required to buy this medicine.
3. Instructor conducts a brainstorming activity.
4. List some of the instructor's favorite OTC products by name brand on the board.
5. Ask: "What are your favorite OTC product names?" List students' responses on the board.

NOTE: If the topic arises, explain the difference between the name of a product and the name brand of a product, for example, aspirin – the product name Vs. Bayer – a brand name for aspirin.

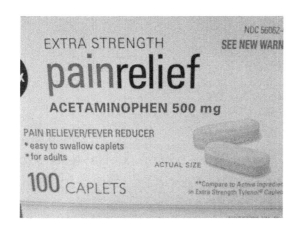

aspirin

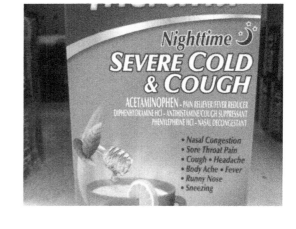

cold medicine

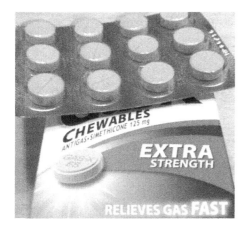

antacid tablets

throat lozenges

pharmacist

pharmacy

UNIT 6 – MEDICAL - LESSON 3 – AT THE PHARMACY
STUDENT BOOK PAGE 98

Time to Speak

A. Complete *To Do First*.
   - Introduce the conversation At the Pharmacy under Time to Speak. Have students repeat each line after the instructor. Repeat each line 5-6 times. Strive for a normal, conversational tone rather than an oral reading tone.
   - Use backward build up for sentences longer than 4 words. Remember to divide sentences into their sound units.
   - Use correct intonation, stress, and rhythm patterns. Include the following intonation patterns:
   - Statement (the voice starts higher and moves downward like going down a staircase through each sound unit in a statement. When the end of the statement is reached, at the period, the voice falls).
   - YES/NO Question intonation pattern for tag question, for example, "Aspirin?"

B. Have students complete *To Do Second.* Call on individual students to read the conversation after each substitution has been drilled.

Time to Speak

To Do First: Repeat the conversation after the instructor.

At the Pharmacy

Speaker A: Customer/Patient   Speaker B: Pharmacist/Store Clerk

1.A.   Excuse me. I have **a headache**. What can I take?
   1.B. You can take **aspirin**.
2.A.   **Aspirin**?
   2.B.   Yes. **Aspirin** is on **Aisle 3**.
3.A.   Thank you.

To Do Second: Speak with a partner. Change the <u>underlined words</u> in the conversation for the Substitutions in No. 1-3 below.

Substitution No. 1
1.A.   Excuse me. I have **a cold**. What can I take?
   1.B.   You can take **cold medicine**.
2.A.   **Cold medicine**?
   2.B.   Yes. **Cold medicine is on Aisle 4.**
3.A.   Thank you.

Substitution No. 2
1.A.   Excuse me. I have **a sore throat**. What can I take?
   1.B.   You can take **throat lozenges**.
2.A.   **Throat lozenges?**
   2.B.   Yes. **Throat lozenges are on Aisle 2**.
3.A.   Thank you.

Substitution No. 3.
1.A.   Excuse me. I have **a stomachache**. What can I take?
   1.B.   You can take **antacid tablets**.
2.A.   **Antacid tablets**?
   2.B.   Yes. **Antacid tablets are on Aisle 6**.
3.A.   Thank you.

UNIT 6 – MEDICAL - LESSON 3 – AT THE PHARMACY
STUDENT BOOK PAGE 99

Grammar Foundation

A. Introduce the Grammar Foundation by reading the information under Using Can and Can't; Could and Couldn't.

B. Complete _To Do_ by having students repeat each example sentence after the instructor. Repeat each one 2-3 times.

C. Ask students for additional examples of sentences using CAN YOU and COULD YOU for polite requests or permission to do something.

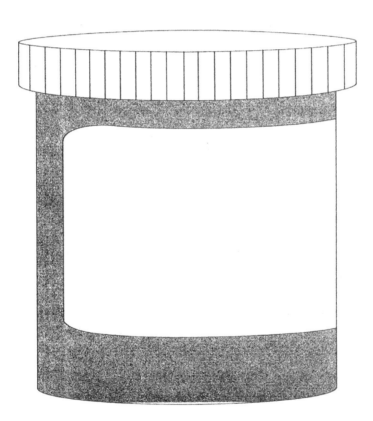

Grammar Foundation

Using Can and Can't; Could and Couldn't

We use CAN for ability and possibility. I am able to or it is possible for me to do something. For example:
- I can play the piano.
- You can take aspirin.
- They can take cough syrup.
- I can teach English.
- We can ask the pharmacist about cold medicine.
- John can't go to the party.

We use COULD for the past, for example:
- When I was young, I could run fast.
- Yesterday I could understand everything the teacher said.
- Last night I couldn't sleep.

Also, we use CAN YOU and COULD YOU to ask questions in the present or future tense. We use either CAN or COULD when we want to ask if something is possible to do, to make a polite request, or to ask permission to do something. For example:
   Ask if something is possible to do
- Can I take aspirin for a headache?
- Could I take pain pills for a backache?
- Could he take antacid tablets for a stomachache?

   Make a polite request
- Could you tell me how to get to Pines Baptist Church?
- Can I have chocolate, please?
- Can I speak to your brother?
- Could I borrow your book?

   Ask permission to do something
- Could Johnny go to the beach with us?

To Do:
Repeat each example sentence after the instructor.

UNIT 6 – MEDICAL - LESSON 3 – AT THE PHARMACY
STUDENT BOOK PAGE 100

A. Introduce Using HAVE to Describe Physical Ailments by reading the information.

B. Have students repeat the example sentences. NOTE: Draw attention to the use of HAS for the third person simple present tense.

<u>Let's Practice</u>

A. <u>Conduct the Let's Practice Activity 1. Can & Can't Listening</u>.
   1. Introduce the activity by reading the instructions under *To Do.*
   2. Demonstrate how to complete the activity by reading the first sentence.
   3. Read each sentence 3 times.
   4. Go over student responses.

Answer Key – answers underlined

1. Juan [can / can't] find his throat lozenges.

2. Carol [**can** / can't] take cold medicine for her cold.

3. Ted [**can't** / can] take aspirin because he is allergic.

4. Where [<u>can</u> / can't] I find antacid tablets?

5. [**Can** / Cans] John take pain pills for a headache?

6. "When [**can** / cans] I take some aspirin?" Tommy asked.

7. [Can't **/ Can**] Marie have a throat lozenge?

8. Ted [**can't** / can] take antacid tablets for his headache.

Using HAVE to Describe Physical Ailments

We use HAVE to describe a physical ailment which a person possesses.

Affirmative Statements

Subject + Have/Has + Object

I	have	a cold.
You	have	a sore throat.
She	has	a stomachache.
He	has	a backache.
We	have	headaches.
They	have	broken arms.

Let's Practice

1. Can & Can't Listening Activity

Listen to the sentences. Circle the correct the word you hear [in brackets] to complete the sentence.

1. Juan [can / **can't**] find his throat lozenges.

2. Carol [can / can't] take cold medicine for her cold.

3. Ted [can't / can] take aspirin because he is allergic.

4. Where [can / can't] I find antacid tablets?

5. [Can / Cans] John take pain pills for a headache?

6. "When [can / cans] I take some aspirin?" Tommy asked.

7. [Can't / Can] Marie have a throat lozenge?

8. Ted [can't / can] take antacid tablets for his headache.

UNIT 6 – MEDICAL - LESSON 3 – AT THE PHARMACY
STUDENT BOOK PAGE 101

B. Conduct the Let's Practice Activity 2. Medicine Mixer
  1. Prepare in advance. Create a set of 3x5 cards. Half the cards will have illness statements, for example: "I have a cold." The other half of the cards will have medicine statements, for example: "You can take cold medicine." Use the statements from the conversation.
  2. Distribute cards to students.
  3. Have students walk around to find the match for their card.
  4. Students read matches to the class.

C. Conduct the Let's Practice Activity 3. At the Pharmacy Role Play
  1. Set up a pharmacy inside the classroom. Draw shelves on the board.
  2. Prepare in advance by gathering a variety of OTC medicines. Alternately, copy the medicine bottle template and write the medicine names on the bottles, for example, 'aspirin'. Use tacky tape or blue painter's tape to affix the bottles to the board on the shelves you've drawn.
  3. Divide students into pairs.
  4. Student 1 is the customer and Student 2 is the pharmacist.
  5. The customer asks the pharmacist for advice for a headache. The pharmacist tells the customer what medicine to take and points it out on the shelves.
  6. Reverse roles.
  7. Continue until all pairs have been the customer and the pharmacist.

D. Conduct the Let's Practice Activity Beat the Cat
Note this is the biblical principle.
  1. Play Beat the Cat with the puzzle sentence: Jesus healed a blind man by spitting on his eyes. See the Activity Bank for instructions how to prepare and play Beat the Cat.
  2. After solving the puzzle, read the story from Mark 8:22-25 to the class.
  3. Read again, this time inviting the students to read aloud with the instructor.
  4. The instructor may choose to comment on the story.

See next page for story...

2. Medicine Mixer

1. The instructor will give each student a card. Half of the cards have illnesses, for example: 'I have a cold'. The other half of the cards will have the medicines, for example: 'You can take cold medicine'.
2. Students walk around to find the match for their card.
3. Read matches to the class.

3. At the Pharmacy Role Play

1. The instructor will set up a pharmacy inside the classroom.
2. Students work in pairs.
3. Student 1 is the customer and Student 2 is the pharmacist.
4. The customer asks the pharmacist for advice for a headache. The pharmacist tells what medicine to take and where to find it in the store.
5. Student 1 looks for the medicine on the shelves.
6. Change roles: Student 1 is the pharmacist and Student 2 the customer. Repeat until all students have been the customer and the pharmacist.

4. Play Beat the Cat
To Do First:

1. This game is like the TV show Wheel of Fortune. The instructor will put a puzzle on the board.
2. Students take turns guessing consonants.
3. If the consonant is in the puzzle, the instructor will write it on the line. If the consonant is NOT in the puzzle, the instructor will draw part of a cat.
4. Continue until only vowels are left in the puzzle.

To Do Second:
Listen to the instructor read the story.

To Do Third:
Read the story out loud with the instructor.

UNIT 6 – MEDICAL - LESSON 3 – AT THE PHARMACY
STUDENT BOOK PAGE 102

Jesus Healing the Blind Man with Spit Mark 8:22-25:
They came to Bethsaida, and some people brought a blind man and begged Jesus to touch him. He took the blind man by the hand and led him outside the village. When he had spit on the man's eyes and put his hands on him, Jesus asked, "Do you see anything?" He looked up and said, "I see people; they look like trees walking around." Once more Jesus put his hands on the man's eyes. Then his eyes were opened, his sight was restored, and he saw everything clearly.

Review Exercises

1. Answer the Questions with Complete Sentences

Answer Key – answers in bold

1. John has a cold. What can he take?
   ___***He can take cold medicine.***___
2. My son has a stomachache. What can he take?
   ___**He can take antacid tablets.**___
3. I have a sore throat. What can I take?
   ___**You can take throat lozenges.**___
4. Mr. Jenkins has a headache. What can he take?
   ___**He can take aspirin.**___

2. Match the Medicine with the Illness.
Write the letter of the illness on the line next to the medicine.

Answer Key – answers in bold

Medicines	Illnesses
1. **C** ___antacid tablets	A. headache
2. **D** ___throat lozenges	B. cold
3. **A** ___aspirin	C. stomachache
4. **B** ___cold medicine	D. sore throat

<u>Mark 8:22-25</u>

They came to Bethsaida, and some people brought a blind man and begged Jesus to touch him. He took the blind man by the hand and led him outside the village. When he had spit on the man's eyes and put his hands on him, Jesus asked, "Do you see anything?" He looked up and said, "I see people; they look like trees walking around." Once more Jesus put his hands on the man's eyes. Then his eyes were opened, his sight was restored, and he saw everything clearly.

Review Exercises

1. Answer the Questions with Complete Sentences

1. John has a cold. What can he take?

___***He can take cold medicine.***_____

2. My son has a stomachache. What can he take?

_____

3. I have a sore throat. What can I take?

_____

4. Mr. Jenkins has a headache. What can he take?

_____

2. Match the Medicine with the Illness.

Write the letter of the illness on the line next to the medicine.

Medicines	Illnesses
1. *C*_____ antacid tablets	A. headache
2. _____ throat lozenges	B. cold
3. _____ aspirin	C. stomachache
4. _____ cold medicine	D. sore throat

Activity Bank

Directions for the activities utilized in the Let's Practice section are included here. In the lesson plans the instructor will sometimes be referred to the Activity Bank for further explanation.

How to Prepare a Concentration Game Board and How to Play Concentration

1. Prepare a Concentration board using a piece of poster board and 4x6 index cards folded to make 24 pockets. Attach the pockets to the board. Number each pocket on the pocket face with a marker.
2. Prepare Concentration cards using 3x5 index cards. Write desired responses on individual cards. For example: questions and answers; split sentences; opposites; vocabulary and definitions, etc. Place one card into each of the Concentration board pockets facing away so the writing on the card cannot be seen.
3. Play begins when a student chooses two cards randomly from the pockets and reads the cards aloud to the class. If a student has chosen a match, i.e. a question and its appropriate answer, the cards are removed from the board and the student receives a point. If the two cards chosen do not match, cards are replaced in the board in the same pocket from which they were taken. Next student plays. Play continues until all cards have been properly matched.
4. At conclusion of play, read all matches aloud.

Prepare Concentration cards using split sentences, word and definitions, vocabulary words and their pictures, etc.

How to Prepare and Play Beat the Cat

1. This game is similar to the TV show "Wheel of Fortune." Write the letters of the alphabet across the top of the board: A-B-C-D…
2. Draw lines to represent the letters of each word in the puzzle sentence. For example:

___ ___ ___   ___ ___   ___ ___ _ ___

3. Students take turns guessing **consonants** only.
4. Fill in the guessed consonants that appear in the puzzle. For example:

___ ___ D   ___ .   L ___ _ ___

5. For consonants guessed that do NOT appear in the puzzle, begin drawing a cat, one body part per incorrect consonant, in the following order: head, body, face, whiskers, ears, tail. The addition of the tail indicates

the teacher has won! Avoid this by adding paws to the cat if needed!

6. Continue until all consonant spaces are filled in.

7. Students guess which vowels fill the remaining spaces in the puzzle. Fill in their correct vowel guesses. For example: G O D I S L O V E

How to Prepare and Play Mix & Match

1. The instructor creates 3x5 card pairs, for example, vocabulary and definition, sentence halves, opposite words, sentence completions, questions and answers, nouns and the adjectives which modify them, etc.

2. Shuffle cards and distribute one per student.

3. Students mix with each other to find their match.

4. Matched pairs share their matches with the class.

How to Play the Add On Game

1. Student 1 makes a statement, for example: "I'm going to the store to buy some apples."

2. Student 2 repeats Student 1's statement and adds his/her own statement, for example, "I'm going to the store to buy some apples and bananas."

3. Continue repeating and adding statements until all have participated.

How to Conduct an Interview Line Up

1. Create two equal lines of students facing each other about 2' apart. Designate Line A and B.

2. Instructor gives an interview topic/question for Line A to interview their partner in Line B.

3. When all have completed the interview, the student at the end of Line A moves to the opposite end of Line A while other students in Line A shift one place over. Line B does NOT move. All students now face a new partner.

4. Instructor gives a new interview topic/question. Line B begins the interview.

5. Continue shifting Line A until all students have interviewed each other.

How to Conduct a Pair, Square, Share Activity

1. Students form pairs and interview each other.

2. Pairs join with another pair.

3. Partners report to the new group what their original partner said.

How to Conduct an Interview Line Up

1. Create two equal lines of students facing each other about 2' apart. Designate Line A and B.

2. Instructor gives an interview topic/question for Line A to interview their partner in Line B.

3. When all have completed the interview, the student at the end of Line A moves to the opposite end of Line A while other students in Line A shift one place over. Line B does NOT move. All students now face a new partner.

4. Instructor gives a new interview topic/question. Line B begins the interview.

5. Continue shifting Line A until all students have interviewed each other.

How to Complete the Mystery Word Search

This activity looks a bit like a cross word puzzle.

Part 1

1. Write fill-in-the-blank sentences using the vocabulary words. Students complete the sentences.

Part 2

2. Create the Mystery Word Search Puzzle. Choose one word to write vertically. Draw a box around this word. Responses to the sentences in Part 1 are written horizontally intersecting the vertical word along a common letter. See example below.

3. Replace the letters of the vertical and horizontal words with blank lines. Write one letter on each line. The vertical word inside the box becomes the mystery word.

4. Students fill in the puzzle with the correct responses from Part 1. The mystery word will appear inside the box.

5. Have students write the mystery word on the line.

Part 1

1. Jesus sat in a **boat**.

2. The man scattered **grain**.

3. Jesus taught a **parable**.

4. The **crowd** was very big.

5. Some **seed** fell on the path.

214

Part 2

```
1.              b  o  a  t
2.        g  r  a  i  n
3.           p  a  r  a  b  l  e
4.  c  r  o  w  d
5.              s  e  e  d
```

Write the mystery word in the box here: **bird**

NOTE: The font used here is Courier New 14 pt. All letters are of equal size so the puzzle lines up perfectly.

How to Teach with the Lipson Method

1. The Lipson Method is a teaching methodology which combines simple sentences with pictures to act as cues to help students recall and retell a story.
2. To create a Lipson lesson, begin by writing a simple story of about 6 sentences. Alternately, summarize a story from a book, newspaper, etc.
3. Illustrate each picture with simple stick figure drawings.
4. Teach each sentence using backward build up, drilling 5-6 times each.
5. Review after every 3 sentences drilled.
6. When all sentences have been learned, ask volunteers to retell the story using the pictures as cues. It is not necessary to repeat the story word for word.
7. Ask comprehension questions about the story.

How to Prepare and Play Bingo

1. Make Bingo cards by photocopying a blank nine-space Bingo grid.
2. Create the items to fill each grid. For example: pictures to represent the vocabulary or sentences in a Lipson story, words or definitions; dates in number form; various time expressions (8:45; quarter to nine); signs (road signs, informational signs), etc.
3.   Put each item on a 1 ½ x 1 ½" yellow Post-It note. Position the Post-It into the blank spaces of a blank nine-space Bingo grid. Photocopy to make an individualized card. Reposition the Post-Its to make different individualized cards.   Alternately, us the computer to create the Bingo grids.

4. To play: distribute a Bingo card and a Smarties candy roll, to be used for Bingo chips, to each student.

5. The instructor calls an item. Students place a candy on the item.

6. When student gets three in a row diagonally, horizontally, or vertically, they call "Bingo!"

7. Check students' answers. Keep score on board.

8. After each round of play, have students clear their cards

Practicing Perfect Pronunciation

Much of English pronunciation is learned through simple repetition. Even the lowest level beginners can learn to hear and recognize the elements of English pronunciation. Therefore, it's helpful if students are introduced to the elements of English pronunciation from the very beginning of their language acquisition. This text emphasizes Sound Units and Intonation Patterns which are discussed below.

As Repetition Drills are foundational for learning to hear and recognize English pronunciation, a review of how to conduct basic drills follows.

Sound Units

Sound units are chunks of words which flow together and are usually said with one breath. The native English speaking listener will naturally recognize Sound Units of spoken English as the speaker will pause for a brief moment between sound units. We can also use grammar to identify sound units.

English words can be divided into two categories: Content Words and Structure (aka Function) Words.

Content Words	Structure Words
Nouns	Articles
Verbs	Demonstratives
Adjectives	Pronouns
Adverbs	Conjunctions
WH-Question Words	Modals
	To Be Verbs

In spoken English, we accent the Content Words and reduce the Structure Words. Sound Units are built around Content Words and their related Structure Words. Students can learn to hear the Sound Units through repetition drills.

Intonation Patterns

Intonation is the rise and fall of the voice. Native English speakers listen for Intonation Patterns to help reinforce the message of the words. The Intonation Patterns introduced in this text are defined below.

Statement – the voice starts higher and moves downward like going down a staircase through each sound unit in a statement. When the end of the statement is reached, at the period, the voice falls. The Statement Intonation Pattern is used for Statements which do not require a response.

We often use arrows drawn on the text to indicate the direction of voice in the Intonation Pattern. For example, here's a simple Statement:

WH-Question – questions that begin with the WH-Question words: Who, What, Where, When, Why, How, require a response from the listener. The voice begins on a high note, then falls through the middle of the sentence until the last Content word when the voice rises to accent the accented syllable in the last Content word and then falls.

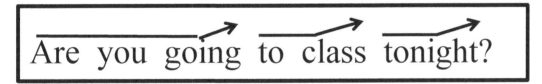

YES/NO Question – questions for which Yes or No are the responses. The voice raises at the end of each Sound Unit and raises dramatically at the end of the sentence.

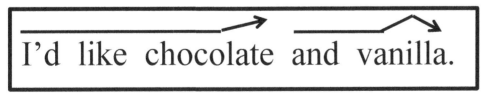

Two Items or Choices Connected with AND – Both items are said with equal stress while the word that connects them, AND, is said at a low pitch.

Conducting Drills

How to Conduct a Repetition Drill

Repetition Drill is used to teach new vocabulary and to teach vocabulary in sentences. To conduct a repetition drill:
1. Show students a picture or object to introduce the vocabulary.
2. Repeat the word 5-6 times while students listen.
3. Students then repeat the word after the instructor 5-6 times.
4. After drilling 3 words, review.

How to use Backward Build up to Teach a Sentence

Sentences are easier to learn by starting at the end of the sentence and working toward the beginning.
1. The instructor repeats the entire sentence one time, for example: There's a Post Office on Main Street.
2. Then the instructor begins with a repetition drill at the end of the sentence with "Main Street."
3. Next, the preposition 'on' is added and the phrase, "on Main Street" is drilled.
4. Third, the beginning of the sentence is drilled, "There's a Post Office".
5. Finally, the entire sentence is drilled, "There's a Post Office on Main Street."

How to Direct Students to Do the Substitution Drill

The Substitution Drill is useful to 'substitute' additional vocabulary words into a sentence that has been drilled already. For example: "There's a **bank** on **New York Avenue**." A conversation then is more useful if Substitute vocabulary is utilized. To indicate the Substitutions, this text uses **bold underlined words.**

How to Conduct a Question and Answer Drill
1. To begin, the instructor models the question by pointing to self to indicate he/she is going to ask the question, and then the instructor asks a question.
2. Instructor then gestures to students to indicate they will answer the question, and then the instructor answers the question he/she has modeled.
3. Instructor continues demonstrating asking the question and answering the question 5-6 times as in a repetition drill.
4. After sufficient modeling, the instructor then conducts the repetition drill. The instructor asks the question, and students answer the question. Drill each question and answer combination 5-6 times.

How to Conduct a Question and Answer Chain Drill

In a Chain Drill, all students practice asking and answering questions.

1. To begin, the instructor asks a question to Student 1 who answers the question.
2. Student 1 then asks a question to Student 2 who answers.
3. Continue the chain until all students have both asked and answered a question.

ABOUT THE AUTHOR

Professor Barbara Kinney Black began her 25 year ESL teaching career as a volunteer in her church, University Baptist, in Coral Gables, Florida. She had taught for just 3 weeks when it became obvious to her that she could do something she loved for a career. She returned to university for a Master's of Science degree in T.E.S.O.L. Since that time she has taught ESL in a diversity of settings including:
Adult Education – Miami-Dade, Florida
College – Miami-Dade College, Miami, Florida - largest college in the U.S.A.
Seminary – New Orleans Theological Seminary - Miami Campus
China – Honghe University - sharing Western ESL teaching technique with Chinese English Teachers

Professor Black has authored ESL curriculum for a variety of applications including:
ESL for Florida Power and Light employees
ESL for employees of Global Mail Solutions
Co-authored <u>Teaching English Techniques & Practice</u> for Honghe University

Professor Black is the author of the multi-level ESL curriculum for adults:
<u>Tried and True ESL Lessons Student</u>
<u>Tried and True ESL Lessons Time Saving Lesson Plans for Instructors</u>
<u>Tried and True Everyday English from Genesis High Beginner and Intermediate ESL Student</u>
<u>Tried and True Everyday English from Genesis High Beginner and Intermediate ESL Instructor</u>

Professor Black enjoys most her involvement, since 1994, as a teacher/trainer for churches in Florida wishing to begin ESL ministries.
Professor Black has directed two ESL ministries in South Florida churches.

Above all, Professor Black delights in seeing her students succeed.

Made in the USA
Columbia, SC
14 November 2021

48912837R00130